MORE

MORE

more

FROM Messes TO Miracles

tammie head

PUBLISHING GROUP
Nashville, Tennessee

dedication

For my Dearest Barbara—

I bet you never dreamed *this* would happen the day you sat listening to the story of a broken girl sitting on your couch so long ago. No one needs to convince us that God transforms messy lives into walking miracles. We are living proof! And should someone suggest running the malls, eating loads of Mexican food, and wasting days away being girls can't serve as catalysts for ushering in redemption—have we got a story to tell! Thank you for clothing me in beautiful dignity. Even in those early days when I was learning how to follow Jesus into my calling, you made sure I was clothed for the call. Because of you I never had to worry when speaking, I was dressed in pretty wares of dignity. . . . What a beautiful crimson thread of redemption the Lord has woven. You are my Naomi. Not only Erin's momma, but mine too. A gift of grace—*Mother of my heart.*

Mess: a situation that is confused and full of problems[1]

Miracle: an extraordinary and welcome event that is not explicable by natural or scientific laws and is therefore attributed to a divine agency[2]

"He got us out of the mess we're in and restored us to where he always wanted us to be. And he did it by means of Jesus Christ." (Rom. 3:23 MSG)

contents

introduction

Messy.

We're all feeling it.

None of us have to stay this way though. God has a miraculous plan for our lives. If I know you like I think I do, *you want it.* So much so, the desire for it probably drives you crazy sometimes. We're each longing for something more.

But I just have to ask—

Have you ever seen something so unbelievable you scratched your head in wonder? And your jaw dropped to the floor? That's what God wants to do in your life. It starts by encountering His presence. Would you like to hear how it happened to me?

I must say: *"I wish my story were prettier."*

Sometimes I prefer a heads-up before stories turn sideways. If you're like me, consider yourself warned.

My life has run the gamut. . . . Going from messy to miraculous, not believing in God to becoming a Christian, self-righteousness to humiliation, religious rule-keeping to enjoying God and, after eighteen years of knowing God, wondering if God was real. Yep, I know about messes. I also know about a God who transforms them.

Miracles are born of God, not methods. Because of this, I'm asking the Miraculous One to throw your eyes back to His realness, love, and presence like never before. Take heart, the *More* you're longing for longs for more of you too.

THE *Lord's* WAY IS TO PUSH US RIGHT INTO THAT *spacious* PLACE WHERE NOTHING IS SURE, BUT ALL IS WELL IN OUR FATHER'S presence. #MORE

chapter one

You were made for MORE

Why not give God your whole life?

I'll tell you why I wouldn't—I was hoping to clean mine up first.

Perhaps you can relate?

The first time I met God, I was in the back room of a Gentlemen's Club. Why those establishments are called Gentlemen's Clubs beats me—I never met a gentleman in one. But let's not go there.

What I'm trying to say is: I wasn't even searching for God when I first heard Him calling me.

I was, however, searching for my face in the mirror to get ready for work. But I was too high to see and squinting wasn't helping. The girl in the mirror—the one struggling to focus—was a kid, really.

I was fifteen years old when I accepted a woman's offer of glitz, glamour, and plenty of money. The woman was right—partly. I got all of those things, but the glitz was cheap, the glamour was trashy, and the money was more than costly. But how else was I to care for myself on a ninth-grade education?

The first night on the job was terrifying. I bawled afterward.

"I can't do this . . . This isn't me."

"Don't worry now, you'll soon toughen up," she comforted.

3

That's when powerful drugs and potent drinks became my best friends. They lent a helping hand for morphing me into someone I wasn't—a stripper.

God spoke only two sentences when He first started drawing me to Him.

"You were made for more," He told me. And then, "Give Me your life."

But how do I give God my life? And why would He want me anyway? And what am I doing here? And who have I become? I hate my life! These people are awful. These men are married! "Go home to your wives! Get away from me!" This is all such a lie. I'm a lie. What do I do? The only Christian I know is Mrs. Kitchen. She's perfect. I can't be her.

My thoughts reacted wildly as if blasted by a bolt of lightning. I'm unsure how much time elapsed before I mustered up the courage to say, "There is no way I can be as perfect as Mrs. Kitchen. My heart is too black."

Desperation landed me here—a place I never imagined as a five-year-old girl pulling my tea sets out among childhood friends to play "tea party."

Maybe carrying those dishes in a black trash bag was symbolic?

God never saw me like trash, but I sure did. Perhaps God saw something similar to what my good friend Jennifer sees when she looks at my two daughters and says, "Now girls, don't ever forget you're fine china." What she means is, "Girls, you are valuable. Now treat yourself as such."

I always smile because, clearly, who doesn't need reminding?

What about you? Can you recall the first time you felt flawed?

Some call it shame—and I do not disagree; but what if it's deeper than shame? What if it's an overwhelming sense of emptiness?

Furthermore, what about this—

Do you often wish your life were better than it is?

Does a subtle longing for something more often gnaw at you?

If you answered "yes," you are not alone.

People everywhere are anguished inside for something *more*. Churched and non-churched alike. I've met them in malls, talked with them in nail shops, prayed with them in my church, encouraged them in my friendships, visited with them at speaking events, cried with them in my home and, honestly, I've been that person myself.

℮〜

When I was younger, I struggled to understand what made life worth the living. Before God saved me, it seemed to me as if life wasn't worth the effort, you know? Restless thoughts tirelessly entertained my mind. I longed for a different version of life and, furthermore, I longed for a different version of me. Deep in my soul's fabric was an irksome sense of void and vacancy.

My momma had me when she was fifteen years old. She was a troubled girl looking for a better situation. I cannot blame her. She ran into the arms of a young man who provided a safe harbor—his momma's house. The marriage crumbled soon after, and my momma returned back home, now with a baby in tow. Many of my childhood memories are of us running to and from that tiny house—trying hard to survive. I probably don't need to tell you that my momma lacked some maternal skills, but I will. Although, let's be honest, who wouldn't? Motherhood is a heavy weight of responsibility for anyone—let alone a young teen.

Due to our conditions, I often cried while asking, "Why don't you love me?"

She'd quickly look away, purse her lips together, and say, "I do. I just don't know how to show it."

Later I would learn for myself—it's hard to offer something you've never received.

To be honest, I've grieved her upbringing nearly as much as my own. Nowadays, I think she would have made a great mom if she were given a different set of circumstances.

I loathe the destroyer's work in my generational line.

I used to think my upbringing was the initiator of my pining for something *more*. But then I grew up and discovered many of my friends felt it too. And their backgrounds were dazzling compared to mine. What I realized is all of us engaged life as human garbage disposals looking for something, *anything*, to whet our appetites and satisfy us.

Some of us sought it in seemingly good ways—pursuing good deeds, being respectable, and passionately watching our every single *p* and *q*. Others sought it in rebellion—pushing the envelope, climbing out windows, and sailing the gusty winds. Neither avenue, respectable or not so respectable, was able to provide what we yearned for.

Truth is, everything sold us short. Finding lasting love. Amassing popularity, power, and control. Working our way up the corporate ladder. Making great money. Having gorgeous bodies. Accumulating loads of material possessions. Owning fabulous homes. Living however, wherever, and with whomever—getting our own way for a change. When our heads hit the pillow at night we each still knew:

Something's missing.

℮〜

Here's what I think.

I think our need for more stems from the same empty well in all of us—even if our attempts to satisfy our emptiness play out differently in each of our lives.

I think this emptiness was created in us *by* God and *for* God.

I think the "more" we're longing for is God.

I hope to prove it to you as our subject matter builds.

Remember the words God spoke over me at the club? *You were made for more.* Those words haunted my growing up. The day I attempted suicide at fifteen, "You were made for more," rang in my ears like fingernails on a chalkboard. I seethed with anger and silently screamed, "Shut up! Who are You anyway?"

To be honest, I felt harassed.

If our paths crossed today, you'd highly doubt this was my experience. My penchant for stylish clothes, polished nails, and for the most part, a happy upbeat personality reveals nothing of my past, but those who knew me "when" say I don't even look the same. My mother-in-law is one of them. She's been most amazed, saying, "God has transformed your entire countenance."

Growing up, there were days and nights I lived terrorized at the hands of several sexual abusers. Anytime opportunity afforded itself, the predators lustfully pounced. One was my grandfather. Unfortunately, I wasn't his only prey. Some in the family yielded to his abusive wiles and did tricks for his money, approval, and manipulative control. I determined early he wasn't getting the same from me. I was young, but I knew it wasn't right. Even in the darkest days, those five words echoed on my insides:

You were made for more.

As a young teen in high school, I decided I couldn't take it anymore. I was done with high school and done with my home life. I was losing my mind. I dropped out of school and married the first guy I could get to marry me. What I didn't foresee is I had only exchanged one nightmare for another. The boy had his own set of problems and you know I had mine. The marriage was a wreck from the beginning, lasting only a matter of months. Though I had biblical reasons to leave, leaving didn't make me better. It set me up for far worse. That's when I tried to commit suicide—drinking poisons and waiting to die, after I beat myself in the face. Only I didn't die. I vomited my guts up as that voice spoke over me, "You were made for more."

In a last-ditch effort to care for myself; I hunted down the crinkly piece of paper. The one with the woman's number on it that promised glitz and glamour and plenty of money. My hands trembled as I dialed her phone, and my voice quivered when I cried for help.

"It's going to be okay," she nicely assured. "You're going to be alright."

Later on I would learn "okay" and "alright" were not so easily attained.

You can take the girl out of the mess. But taking the mess out of the girl?

Part of me wishes you knew me back "when." Back in the days I lied through my teeth and told all sorts of stories. That's what people with my kind of past do. They make stuff up. Somehow it softens the pain while helping to appease the questions of curious people.

Only, it backfires.

Like the time I told my boyfriend, Erin, and his family that my dad was in the Italian mafia. How else was I to explain his absence? The lie seemed believable to me. I did have dark hair, olive skin, a fiery personality, and I loved me some spaghetti and Italian dressing. That counts, right?

All was fine and dandy 'til I walked down the aisle, and they became my kinfolk. Talk about a soul set on edge. That lie haunted me like an evil spirit lingering over my head. Then one day my home telephone rang.

"Hello?" I answered.

"Is this Tammie Mitchell?"

"It is. May I ask who's calling?"

"This is your cousin, Mayola. Do you remember me?"

My stomach leapt to my throat—and sweat drops appeared on my forehead.

"I do . . . I mean, a little. What do you need?"

Somehow she got my number and was calling because our grandmother was dying of cancer, and her last dying wish was to have the opportunity to perhaps talk to me. I quickly informed her under no uncertain terms, "We are not family, and don't you ever call my house again."

Click—I slammed down the phone.

Sadly, our grandmother died. And later I would apologize profusely to Mayola.

But I'm getting ahead of myself.

A year or so after that phone call, I gave my life to Jesus Christ. And that lie? The one about the mafia? God was not letting me off the hook.

"It's time to tell the truth. I want you to find your father. He doesn't know Me, and I want you to take Me to him."

You better know I put up a fight—that's what fear will do to you.

"There's a whole world of people out there! Why can't You send one of them?"

God didn't answer back. In fact, He quit talking altogether.

Did you know God plays the silent game? He does! Except it's not a game to Him. It's a supernatural spanking for anyone who loves feeling close to Him. About three weeks later, I got so lonely for His company I decided bravery was a better option than rebellion.

But, get this—

As if I needed one more reason to obey, my pastor preached a sermon on someone having a "nag." Something nagging at you, something secretive pestering you, something refusing hiddenness because God is laser focused on it and is saying, "Own up. Get it out. Tell the truth. And deal with it."

I cried through the ENTIRE message.

And thought, *Stop it—What if Erin starts thinking you're having an affair?*

After getting home and putting my oldest daughter, Peyton, down for a nap, I tattled on my lying self.

I was shocked when Erin graciously said, "Honey, it's not that big of a deal. I really think you should find your dad."

You've got to be kidding me! Then again, maybe he was flat-out relieved?

Next I had to find the same bravery and courage to call the extended family.

I could kick myself for not cooking an Italian spread for the big reveal. Wouldn't that have been so great? But, no. I was just trying not to vomit. Finally, I nerved up and spit it out. I'll never forget my father-in-law's expression when he said, "That's ALL?" and his shoulders dropped in relief. Or my mother-in-law quipping, "Well, I never believed you anyway."

We laughed our heads off—still do to this day.

Want to hear something awesome?

I felt God's nearness again, and my emptiness subsided.

I learned two valuable lessons that day about God's presence and character.

I learned how much the presence of God is the "more" factor I ultimately long for. I also learned if the Lord keeps insisting integrity on a matter we'd much rather keep hidden, it is for our greatest freedom and joy. The heart of God is never to shame us but to free us.

I hope you know I'm trying to show you what a mess I was. I have a purpose in it, you know. I want you to know whatever your messy situation is, you're not alone. Madness, sadness, unfulfilled longings, and inadequacies? Everybody's got some skeletons in their closet. I just happen to have a graveyard. But that's okay. God brings corpses to life.

I tend to think God has a tender spot for human messiness, anyway.

Now, I'm not saying God enjoys our messes, per se. I can't imagine Him smiling over victimization or broken hearts, nor can I picture Him happy about poverty and injustice or humanity's various illnesses. I am saying I think God finds our messes somewhat attractive because He enjoys showing up, performing a miracle, standing us to our feet, and loving us to life.

I've seen God come where messy and misery meet too many times to deny it.

In fact, I saw it recently while holding a tiny baby girl in my arms. She was an African orphan, three years old, raped repeatedly by a man in her slums—left unable to walk. "She only talks at night," her caretaker said, "telling of her abuses." Anger burned my face, and I bit my lip to keep from screaming, "Where is her victimizer? Let me at him. I'll scratch his eyes out!"

Instead, I took her ravaged body into my arms, and began rocking her back and forth. It's a wonder I didn't suffocate the poor child. Then again, her body was as stiff as a stick. Her limbs refused to relax in my arms. The madness of her situation was too much. I was stricken by a million thoughts, a million emotions, and nausea—I felt sick.

All I could do was all I knew to do—pray. No. I begged.

"God, I beg You. Heal her and pour love from my pores. Do a miracle."

God hears the cry of the desperate—He's listening to our pleas. I wasn't begging for God's help as if He needed convincing. I was only begging for Him to hurry.

Are you ready for something amazing?

She smiled that day . . .

And she walked.

Six months later, she was a completely different child.

That's a walking miracle right there.

I'm not suggesting God shows up like this every time. Experience alone proves otherwise, but I am saying the God I have come to know and love has enjoyed restoring me from my own personal slums.

When God speaks, chaos snaps into order—like cyclones calmed, like dead bones arising, like darkness fleeing, like broken lives made gorgeously whole.

I'm not guessing, *I know*. This is the story of my own life.

Once I was tormented, now I am free.

Once I was blind, but now I see.

Once I survived, now I dream dreams.

With one touch, Jesus of Nazareth, the Saving God, changed my life.

Would you believe after twenty years I am still not who I was?

Oh, I've been a mess a time or two since then. But nothing like the maddening mess I was before I met God, before He opened my eyes.

I was not orphaned like the little girl I was holding, but I grew up within high levels of abusive chaos. Distrust ravaged my bones. I, too, hardly relaxed in anyone's presence—even the seemingly nice folks.

Unlike Baby C, my rescue did not come until many years later.

Which means, I learned the skills of surviving as a happy-faced actress who feverishly toiled at keeping her act together because, indeed, life had become a stage and living out a convincing performance of perfection was of utmost consequence.

For whom, you ask?

Well, it took me years to finally answer this correctly—*myself*.

I was scared of succumbing to what I feared most: Being a good-for-nothing, wimpy and weak, mangled-to-the-core mess.

Like the little orphan I was tightly rocking, only a God of wonders could undo my tangled-up mess of lies and destructive thinking.

And He did—He began the process all by Himself when I was not asking or looking for *anything* religious.

Restoring people is one of the things He does best.

℮⁓

To be honest, few have known my background for plenty of good reasons. Nevertheless, in the winter of 2011, God used a time of healing from surgery to probe my heart about publicly sharing the truth about how He radically changed my life, and where I first met Him. I tend to live at breakneck speed much like everybody. Sometimes the Lord jerks a knot in my neck to get my attention. Admittedly, that's where I was.

It was time to listen, and to listen up carefully.

"Why are you stealing My glory?" He nudged.

I was utterly taken aback. "What do You mean, Lord?"

"Why aren't you telling what I've really done for you?"

I started sobbing.

"God, You know stories like mine aren't so acceptable in church."

For one who grew up in tumultuous waters of uncertainty, I like the land of safety. For a restless wanderer who lived many years full of conflict, suffering, and being eaten alive by vexing hopelessness, I do not like this portion of knowing God, of walking in step with Him. I lived enough years in survival mode—sucking wind, losing my mind, and performing hard. This journey God is calling me to whiffs of danger. As if I'm being asked to step into Daniel's fiery furnace or, as the Israelites, into the raging waters of the Red Sea. Those are fascinating Bible stories to read—but to live? This feels like that. I know it's not, but please throw me a few bones of empathy. I know all will not approve of my background and it's killing the approval addict in me—the one who really does need to die.

But I've also learned a few things about God—

Following God kills *us*—just so you know. In God's economy, dying precedes all living. The Lord's way is to push us up and out of our comfort zones all the way into His strong arms of a thousand dichotomies; rest and risk, safety and unknown, death and life, worship and warfare, wounds and healing, suffering and joy. He pushes us right into that spacious place where nothing is sure, but all is well in our Father's presence.

One reason I had guts enough to write this book was because my hairdresser Tanja helped me get brave. The day I showed up at her shop weary, ready to quit because of all that was at stake, was the day I realized how necessary this message really is. My little fiery Yankee, born-of-Serbian-Orthodox-heritage, transplanted-to-the-South, wielding-a-pair-of-scissors Tanja has cut more than just my hair. She's been a tool in the hand of God to cut away religious junk tangling up my soul. Junk I had no clue was even there.

She looked at me with shock when I mentioned quitting and said, "Tammie, don't you understand you are writing to people like me?"

Tears stung my eyes. I hadn't thought of it that way. She went on to say, "If you're just writing for people like your church friends then, by all means, use a bunch of generalities about your life. But if you're writing to the rest of us, we need to hear what you've shared with me. We're living in the real world. And we need the help—somebody to shoot straight with us. Besides, your life isn't so shocking to us. We get it. We get *you*."

She was right.

God did ink people's junk all over the Bible's pages, right?

So why am I hiding my own? Do I not trust God with my reputation?

Think about it. Paul was Saul, a religious madman. How would you like to be known as one who, among other heinous crimes, gave nod to the killing of the first Christian martyr? And Mary Magdalene, she was demonized! How about that? Miss Rahab. Good grief. Poor thing can't ditch being known as a former prostitute. Then King David—adulterer, liar, murderer. Marriage material, eh? Or Peter who denied the Lord to His face! Is your face grimacing like mine? What about Solomon? Hundreds of wives. Can you imagine? Here's a big one for you: The demoniac of Gadara—he ran around naked scaring the daylights out of people until Jesus miraculously set him free. How's that for weird?

Yes, dysfunction is littered all over the sixty-six books of the Bible.

It reads like a modern-day reality show sans the Jesus factor.

Truth is, when I read people's life stories, I'm encouraged or, at the least, forewarned. Aren't you? I cannot help but to rejoice over their victories and take notes of their mistakes. Who doesn't love when a captive is set free? I want to live just like them! Who cares about their background? I love their faith! Who's focusing on their junk? I'm focusing on their God!

I hope my junk makes you see my God.

At the end of the day these are the questions I've wrestled with:

- *Is God happy about our silence?*
- *What if our silence is keeping us messy?*
- *If God wrote our life into the pages of Scripture how would it read?*
- *If this notion scares us, could it be time to let God redeem our messes?*

I'm not suggesting we throw everything out there for the world to see—even I haven't done that. But I am asking this: Do people know how good your God has been to you?

Is your whole life—good, bad, and ugly—surrendered into His hands?

These days I am resigned to go with God. Even if it kills me.

Could He be calling you to do the same?

I'm not talking about going to church more.

I'm not talking about doing another Bible study.

I'm not talking about listening to another podcast.

I'm not talking about attending another small group or reading another God-book.

I'm talking about throwing ourselves at Jesus' feet and surrendering our guts out—messiness and all—to the One who promises to fulfill us beyond our imaginations.

℮⁓

Friend, what is your mess right now? Has tragedy struck you or someone you love? Are you in a season of personal crisis and need a miracle? Are you feeling worthless and rejected? Are you down in the dumps and you don't know why? Does an addiction have you or someone you love enslaved? Has a relationship gone awry? Is your health under attack?

Many of us are in troubling situations we don't understand, nor do we know where to go from here. We can't see past our present disappointments, confusions, and despair because, in all honesty, we never saw ourselves traveling down this broken, fragile road.

Struggles can have a crippling effect on us, leaving us empty and wondering, *What happened to my legs? Will I ever recover? Will I get back up?*

I have good news for you. You will. You can. How do I know?

Because I'm standing.

If you're ready to find what you're longing for, you've come to the right place. If you have an itch you can't seem to scratch, keep reading. If you're wrestling with bouts of loneliness, worthlessness, and hopelessness, I've got good news. If you're feeling like you have no purpose, overwhelmed with life, and dying for a change, I think God has a word for you.

My prayer for you is similar to my prayer for the little orphan girl. I am asking God to do a miracle in your life—a now miracle, where you experience His loving presence in the deepest crevices of your soul. Places you cannot quench no matter how hard you've tried.

If you'll lend me your ear, this is a message on how to find your spiritual legs.

To start walking. To start running. To start living the miraculous life.

You were made for more than mere survival.

So why not give God your whole life?

ARE YOU WILLING TO

THROW DOWN

YOUR CRUTCHES OF
SELF RELIANCE

TO GIVE *God* WHAT HE *wants?*

HE WANTS *your Life.*

#MORE

chapter two

a MeSSY miraculous collision

The day God's Spirit peeled back the invisible veil separating the seen from the unseen was the day my life was ruined forever—gloriously ruined. All at once, I was slayed by God's beauty. Undone by my sinfulness. Touched by God's kindness. And lavished in God's love. I had a hunch there was more to knowing God—but this?

Crumbling before His majesty in surrender felt almost compulsory-like. It seemed I could not help myself. Nor did I want to—and why would I? God was lovely and kind; sweetest love divine, and so staggeringly impressive. Thinking about it now, two decades later, I want to drop my head and bawl.

Sadly, some of us have believed at one time that Christianity (religion) is for "weak and wimpy people" who need a "crutch." Nowadays I realize nothing could be further from the truth. Truth is, giving our life to God is quite brave since, in doing so, we actually ditch our own crutches of self-sufficiency; we quit trying to do life on our own temporary props.

I'd like to suggest that surrendering our lives to our Maker in trust is one of the most daring and risky things we can do. Christianity is *not* a faith made up of wimps. Just ask any serious worshipper of Christ if following God requires us to have some supernatural backbone to us, and they'll surely agree. Keeping the faith by walking in step with the Holy Spirit is no cakewalk, I assure you. Neither is standing strong from day to day.

Believe me, I know.

Remember the fifteen-year-old girl? The one in the mirror, struggling to focus? I wasn't ready to give God my life, but I couldn't pull myself together enough to work either. So I gathered up my things and left. This same scenario of going to work, trying to get ready, feeling sickened, and returning back home played out repeatedly 'til I was flat broke. After a while, I panicked.

What is happening to me? Why can't I work anymore? What am I going to do?

I was clueless to the truth: God was working a miraculous plan to rescue my life. Later I'd discover how fearing God, fearing my future, and this new disgust inside of me for the job were the precise ingredients God was using to change my life forever.

While I wasn't ready to come clean with God, I did feel a sense of urgency to come clean to my boyfriend's mother. I couldn't get talking to her off my mind. A huge chunk of my heart longed for honesty—to fess up to my messed-up life. Guilt piled up on me for hiding what I did for a living from her. Not only did I feel guilty, I was growing increasingly nervous of her somehow finding out.

By now, her son and I had dated well over a year. She believed I worked at a country western bar and, honestly, I was not Mrs. Head's first pick for her son. When a boy's momma is not that into you, you know it. *And I knew it.* But who could blame her?

In the end, Mrs. Head was the only decent woman around at the time, and I really longed for a woman to talk to. I felt like she wouldn't at all understand where I was coming from. But, then again, what did I have to lose? She already didn't like me.

I figured maybe, just maybe, my honesty would at least usher in some respect.

I bit my nails to the quick while driving to her house.

Once Erin left to ride his four-wheeler, I nervously situated myself on her couch and proceeded to open a can of worms. If she was shocked at hearing unfiltered details of incest, physical abuse, family betrayal, a lifestyle of drugs, rebellion, and a broken marriage, she showed no signs of it. Looking back, I'm unsure how she kept her composure learning her son's girlfriend was such a train wreck, but she did. The woman was strong, I tell you. She still is to this day.

Would you believe, days later, Mrs. Head called and invited me to lunch? *She sure did.* Believe it or not, that one day of lunch turned into several times a week. It was foreign to me, but I drank it up. Since I worked nights, my days were open, and she only worked part-time.

She and I talked a mile a minute over chips and salsa, and I told her *everything.* So much so, I cannot help but to grin. Let's just say: I was the youngest but she was the most naive. June Cleaver had no idea she signed up for a schooling. Neither did my stray-cat-self know I had signed up for a momma. I fell in love with Miss Barbara in those days and she fell in love with me. The memories of those days are like golden treasures tucked within my heart—such gifts to me.

Another thing we did was tear up the malls. Oh my, did we *ever* have a blast.

My family hardly had a pot to pee in growing up, much less the means to shop at mall stores. Let's just say, I was prouder than a peacock carrying shopping bags to the car from Express, Foley's, and New York & Company. I'll not mention the sizable shopping addiction I'd need God to help me overcome later on down the road—no, no. For now, Barbara was clothing my rag-tattered soul in dignity, and loving my deadened heart to life. And I think God was smiling too.

Unbeknownst to me, Barbara and her two sisters were formulating a plan to rescue me from my job.

The day Barbara told me to quit working was the greatest day of my entire life. Recalling it now brings tears to my eyes. I couldn't believe someone would fight for my future and give me a hand up. It felt like a fairy tale come true since I had lived entirely tormented that I'd never be anything more than what I was, and loathed life. Thoughts like, *Where will I be when I'm forty? Will I still be stuck in this madness?* played in my mind obsessively.

I'll have you know: *I'm forty today.*

Had someone told me, "You'll be a Bible teacher by the time you are forty. You'll also travel the United States teaching people about Jesus, as well as in Zambia, Africa. Not only that, you will also be a published author who writes materials to help people know God more." I'd have said, "Are you talking to me? Oh no . . . you have the wrong girl!"

I imagine during all that time I wasted being freakishly afraid of my future, God was thinking, *You just wait, child, I have something up My sleeve that is going to blow your mind. You'll never guess what life will be like for you at forty, or how I'm planning to use this whole messy situation. Not only for your good but also for My glory. If you only knew how I plan on taking that stage of degradation you despise and flipping it into a platform that offers hope—it'd blow your mind.*

But I'm getting a little ahead of myself.

Let's back up to me finally working a legit job.

Oh the joy I felt when Barbara's sister, Connie, helped me get a job at her law office in downtown Houston. I felt so official in my professional clothes and pumps, working for an attorney. Never mind that I hardly could type, and it took me f-o-r-e-v-e-r. I answered to Connie and she graced my inadequacies. Running paperwork to the courthouse was my favorite. I was totally digging my job. Is this how normal feels? Someone pinch me!

When the line turned pink on the pregnancy test a month later, I was shocked. I knew how this happened, mind you, but how do we tell *this* to Erin's parents? I'll never forget the phone call, listening to Erin tell them we needed to talk. I'll also never forget sitting back down on that old familiar couch with a new confession.

His daddy paced the floor and his mother talked fretfully. After what seemed like an eternity, Erin and I took to the door with a game plan. We'd soon have a baby. His parents would help us. And everything would work out just fine—they were certain of it! But there was one stipulation: *We had to get married.*

Oh man. That one stipulation posed a serious problem . . .

In all those conversations telling Barbara *everything*, I'd held something back.

I was still married to the other guy.

And I didn't have the heart to tell her now. Truth is, I kept meaning to take care of it. Never did I think anything like this would happen.

So what's one to do in such a perplexing a situation like this?

I'm unsure what you would do but this is what I did: I commenced to acting terribly scared of getting married a second time by saying I wasn't sure, that I had to think about it. Then I hightailed it out of there with a made-up mind to head to the library early the next morning to check-out a book—a book on how to get a divorce. Listen, I may have qualified as uneducated but I certainly wasn't stupid. Everything I needed to know was in a book somewhere, and I was not only determined to find it, I was determined to execute it. Those Heads had been far too good to both of us to let them down now.

Within a few months, I took care of business and we announced to his folks we were, "Ready to get married!" Barbara helped me plan the wedding, and Erin and I were husband and wife before our little baby arrived.

Want to hear something astounding?
We just celebrated twenty-two years of marriage.
Can you even believe?
God has been unmistakably good to us.

I sure wish we could sit and talk right now. I'm unsure what you'd want to say to me, but I already know what I'd want to say to you: Please don't think for a second my life is mess-free because it is *not*. And just because God has moved mountains in my life does not mean He hasn't also left some mountains unmoved. I'll tell you more about this as we journey ahead, but for now I want you to know this: Not only do I need Jesus as much as you, I need His presence just as much too.

More than anything, what I hope you're hearing, elevated above anything I am sharing is—there is a God who considers *every* life worthy, not just the good folks. God loves a ramshackle soul just as much as He loves a Mother Teresa soul. He plays no favorites. Jesus died for the good, the bad, and the very ugly.

Now some might find this irksome, to think God loves a murderer as much as a religious rule keeper; but I don't. Sinners who've drank of the cup of the sweet grace of God hope all get an opportunity to drink too. Even those whose track record looks nothing like our own.

The glorious Good News is *whosoever* will "come" are beckoned to take their places before a gracious God who longs to lavish all of us *personally* in His generous, redeeming love. All stand side by side at the foot of the cross, no one more worthy than the other. For the Lord says, "Come, everyone who is thirsty, come to the waters; and you without money, come, buy, and eat! Come, buy wine and milk without money and without cost! . . . Seek the LORD while He may be found; call to Him while He is near. Let the wicked one abandon his way and the sinful one his thoughts; let him return to the LORD, so He may have compassion on him, and to our God, for He will freely forgive" (Isa. 55:1, 6–7).

Can you see? It's not about us. It's all about Him.

Oh, Him. The One who lovingly says, *Will you trust?*

❧

Speaking of trust—

Three months after Erin and I married, the most delicate and darling little bundle of baby girl was entrusted into our care, Miss Peyton LeeAnn Head. And, boy, God would use that child to transform our lives forever.

The doctor handed her to Erin first so he could finish tending to me. I knew Erin was going to make the best daddy when I watched him cradle Peyton in his arms. He kept whispering to her, "You're so beautiful, you're so beautiful," as a stream of tears ran down his cheeks.

Now me, on the other hand—I was scared stiff.

When I looked into her face for the first time, I was unexpectedly terrified. I didn't know I was having a girl. We chose to be surprised. And, man, was I ever. Something about having a girl scared me to death. How would I keep from messing her up with all my baggage and no healthy well to draw from?

In that moment, somehow I knew I needed God.

❧

Peyton's arrival came five months before a devastating death in our family. My brother-in-law (Erin's sister's husband) suddenly died of cancer. When he lay dying, he kept saying, "The light is so bright, and the music is so loud." Except there were no lights on and no music was playing. It was the middle of the night, and the room was pitch black. His wife encouraged him to go back to sleep, and she did too. She never dreamed she'd wake up to him lying beside her dead the following morning.

Talk about devastating!

But God used Peyton's birth and Jesse's death as a wake-up call for me: *This God who wanted my life was getting it.*

I didn't just need God for Peyton because I was a momma now. I needed God for *me.* The thought of dying and going to hell terrified me. Even more, if heaven was real, then I wanted to be counted in.

And if I could help it, God was getting the rest of the family too.

So I commenced to round us all up for church.

In those days, our only association with church was Erin's great-uncle who was a longtime deacon at the First Baptist Church of Houston. He hadn't attended in years due to age, but there was a sense of security going to such a long-standing congregation.

I'll never forget that first Sunday. The size of the church was intimidating, but the pastor was a robust, jovial man who seemed friendly. They called him Brother John Bisagno, and I liked how he preached. When he wrapped up his message, he invited those who wanted to "receive Jesus" to step into the aisle, and to come forward to talk to someone who would be there to receive us.

So I did it. I walked the aisle. And within a few weeks—I got baptized.

I attended four weeks of Sunday morning classes on the faith.

And "played church" for two years—all to no avail.

I was baffled. I kept thinking, *Where is this God who wanted my life?*

I knew there was more, but I couldn't quite understand how to get it. I was doing all of the outward motions the church people were saying to do, but nothing was working.

I would read the Bible and it was like reading another language. It infuriated me. I was an avid reader but couldn't get this book. I'd read a sentence or two, and then look away while trying to articulate to myself what I'd just read. Nothing. My mind was entirely blank. I remembered zilch.

I'd think to myself, *This book is weird. It's almost like it's another language.*

Looking back, I was right, it *was* another language—a spiritual one.

One writer of the Scriptures puts it this way: "People who aren't spiritual can't receive these truths from God's Spirit. It all sounds foolish to them and they can't understand it, for only those who are spiritual can understand what the Spirit means" (1 Cor. 2:14 NLT).

Yep, I agree. That book was just plain weird.

❧

Though I struggled in school and eventually dropped out, I had a passionate love for reading. God must have planted this in me because I come from a long line of high-school dropouts, and reading was never anybody's thing.

I can remember being a little girl, living in a tiny town in Missouri for a time. I'd walk to the local library all by myself, feeling so big in my britches. I'd check out all kinds of books, returning home with arms sore from carrying that heavy brown paper bag. I can't recall ever reading a single one; they probably weren't even on my level. But I do remember loving how they felt, and smelled, and made me feel exceptionally smart.

So when God brought two Christians into our lives who loved us well, and created a safe space for us to ask questions, I had to ask about that book—*the Bible.* Curtis's response to my question was simple but profound: "Pray to God before you read it, and ask Him to open your eyes."

Hmmm. That was a new thought.

Curtis worked for Mr. Head, and though he was plenty of years older than Erin, he took a liking to him—even inviting Erin and I to join he and his wife, Julie, for dinner. The thought of hanging out with them intimidated me at first. They were religious and we were not, but Erin insisted I had nothing to worry about; and he was right.

I was puzzled by their love for us because Erin and I were clearly different from them. I still cussed like a sailor, smoked cigarettes like a freight train, and lived like a hellion even though I was now searching for God. And when they loved us instead of judging us, I noted these people were peculiar. They didn't hide their own mistakes. In fact, they shared them freely. I admired their flagrant authenticity and honesty, and I loved being with them. In fact, on nights when they asked us to dinner we'd often pull back into their driveway afterward only to end up sitting outside in their van for an hour or more talking. As if we had not gotten enough of each other? It was during these times that I began asking questions about God and Christianity. I liked their answers. They intrigued me, and I thought back on them quite often.

One weekend in October of 1994 they invited us to a prayer gathering at their church. Erin was not as crazy about using up his Friday night or most of his Saturday but somehow I convinced him to attend it with me, and his best friend, Jeff, for that matter. Neither one of those two slackers seemed very interested that Friday night, but I sure was.

On the ride home, Jeff made a statement that got he and I to arguing—"If you know God it doesn't mean you have to walk with Him every single day."

I didn't know much. But I knew Jeff was dead wrong. So I reasoned back, "Why would someone *not* walk close to God every day if they know Him?"

The notion of someone knowing God as a personal Savior, but not desiring to live particularly close to Him each day perplexed me. Is it not a relationship after all? And aren't relationships, by nature, relational?

To be honest, what did either of us know? We were both heathens.

My poor husband. He just sat there enduring our religious nonsense.

The following morning, we showed back up at the church, and the atmosphere was energetic and happy, people bustling back and forth. First we attended a big session, then a smaller lecture of our choosing. I took plenty of notes, and drank up the various teachings. In all, I was burning inside to find God like all of the others.

But how? Was there more?

Once the lectures wrapped up, everybody gathered together before going home. They had us group into small circles and hold hands while closing the conference out in prayer.

My group commenced to doing it and—*bam*.

A furious hunger for God overtook me. I began begging God to know Him, to find Him. If there was more, I wanted it. I bore my guts in desperation to Him like never before.

Then, *whoosh*.

God's presence overtook me. Unlike anything I've experienced before or have since then. Encountering the fullness of the presence of God was breathtakingly unbelievable. And, like I've told you, my only response to His Majesty was a compulsive, devastating, unreserved surrender. I finally let this God who wanted my life all the way in.

Take my life. Take all of me. I am Yours forever.

A different girl left that church than the one who entered. My darkened heart was transformed into gorgeous color— just like that. The first gush of God's abiding presence inside my heart was beyond my wildest imagination. Never before had I felt such love! Never before had I felt such peace! Never before had I felt such joy!

When I encountered Jesus, I fell hard and fast in love with Him. Jesus was not just a Jewish man of history long ago who claimed to be God—no, no. Jesus was alive and utterly mind-blowing.

Now, get this—

Would you believe Jeff gave his life to Christ too? And would you also believe he works in ministry? That boy ended up going to Bible college and everything.

How's that for walking with Jesus every day?

e~

Later that same day, we had plans with our friends for the night. As we sat on the back porch, I smoked a cigarette and shared what Jesus had just done in my life. Every time I'd tell her something about God, I'd look down at the Bible in my lap and see exactly what I was talking about on the page. It was nuts! I'd just about holler trying to tell her, "Girlfriend, this must be God talking to you! I don't know the Bible!" as I proceeded to read her the verse. I'd later understand this is the leadership of God's Spirit within His people. But for now, I was simply overjoyed by the reality of God's nearness in my life.

And remember my angst for understanding the Bible?

Oh my. That cigarette was not the only thing lit on fire on the back porch that night. God lit a consuming fire in my soul for His Holy Scriptures. Not only did I fall in love with God, I fell in love with His Word. All I wanted was to bury my nose in it for hours and hours a day and talk with God about what I was reading. So much so, I was on pins and needles every weekday morning because I wanted Erin to skedaddle to work so I could be alone in God's Word; reading and praying and enjoying God.

I must admit, those in my world hardly knew what to think of me. Not my husband, not my closest friends, not even myself, actually. Suddenly, I didn't think like myself anymore. I didn't talk like myself anymore. I didn't act like myself anymore.

Who cleaned up my mouth?

And where was this bravery to talk so freely about Jesus coming from?

I had become a walking miracle.

In fact, my dear friend who helped me to learn more about God felt like I zoomed right past her spiritually. Because I lacked understanding about the spiritual life, I didn't get that I had somehow hit the fast track. I only knew I wanted more of Jesus. That's it.

But that's not all.

I wanted so much for people to know Jesus, too, everywhere I went.

In fact, one time I got so excited talking about Jesus, I talked to the Subway guys for several hours after stopping in to pick up a sandwich. No biggie that I told my husband, while leaving Wednesday night church, that I'd see him at home in a few minutes. Or that the time was now 11 o'clock at night, and I did not have a cell phone back then. Oh man, when my husband walked into the Subway, after backtracking my drive home, he was madder than a hornet. I can still recall his tone when he looked at me and said, "What in the world are you doing? You've had me worried sick. Get home."

Once home I tried so hard to justify it, "But, honey, they were *really* into hearing about Jesus." But he wasn't buying it. He only replied, "Yeah, more like they were into *you*."

I was incensed.

Thankfully, I wised up soon after to realize he was right. His wifey here needed a large dose of knowledge added to her cyclone of zeal. But do cut me some slack.

Walking in the light never felt so good.

Nowadays I wish I could offer my heart on loan for a day to those who haven't yet experienced the joy of knowing God personally—especially those who mock and sneer—so they could sit with God awhile. Surely they'd change their minds in the presence of such a wonderful, redeeming love. After twenty years of knowing Him, I can still say: Nothing compares to knowing God intimately through His Son Jesus Christ—*nothing*.

Whether we've grown up in church, or grown up in the most godless dysfunction this side of heaven, you and I need Jesus' salvation. We need Him to secure our eternal destinies, and we also need His help to live a godly life. Religious practices, no matter how high and lofty, never fully satisfy. *We need Jesus*. In fact, if church attendance and living a devout life are not drawing us closer to His presence in increasing intimacy, I'd say we're being cheated and, sadly, many of us are. This is why so many struggle with restlessness, both inside and outside the walls of religion.

We are all craving the presence of God.

Much deeper than relational messes, physical messes, emotional messes, and financial messes, is the universal mess of mankind; and this mess cannot be sidestepped if we're planning on finding our legs, and getting on to living the free life God has for us. Our biggest mess has to do with our sinful nature. For God Himself says, "There is no one righteous, not even one. There is no one who understands; there is no one who seeks God. All have turned away; all alike have become useless. There is no one who does what is good, not even one. . . . For all have sinned and fall short of the glory of God" (Rom. 3:10–12, 23).

Now I know in our modern society we don't like old-fashioned words like *sin*. But if we're going to work on allowing God to fashion us into walking miracles, we better also work on being honest. And the first place of exposure is right here. We must come into agreement with God by admitting we are a sinful people in need of a Savior. Now . . . and every single day.

Friend, the same God who faithfully pursued me is pursuing you.

The question is: Are you willing to throw down your crutches of self-reliance to bravely give God what He wants? He wants your life. There comes a time when what's holding us back from Him needs to get dropped—the fear, the shame, the rebellion, and the unbelief.

The Lord wants to offer us His life-changing hope, but we must be brave enough to lift up our eyes, to throw open our hearts, and to receive what He's longing to place in our hands. He has spoken so clearly through His Word, "'For I know the plans I have for you,' says the LORD. 'They are plans for good and not for disaster, to give you a future and a hope'" (Jer. 29:11 NLT).

But the Lord very rarely forces Himself on us. He graciously extends His invitation like a loving Father by saying, "'In those days when you pray, I will listen. If you look for me wholeheartedly, you will find me. I will be found by you,' says the LORD" (Jer. 29:12–14 NLT).

Indeed, the Gentlest Man of gentlemen simply bids us to, "*Come.*"

No matter what you've done, "*Come.*"

No matter what your messy state is, "*Come.*"

No matter how you've run, "*Come.*"

Did you know you can come to the Father just as Erin and I went to his parents?

Confess your mess, child. Not only will He show you His love for you in the midst of it, but He will also show you His achieving power to fully take care of it. Don't you worry. Don't you fret. His only stipulation is that you give Him your life, and trust . . .

TRUE faith

BEGINS AND ENDS WITH

GOD

AS THE *grand* SUBJECT.

transformation

OUT OF ANY MESS ONLY COMES

WHEN WE FIX OUR EYES

ON

CHRIST.

#MORE

chapter three
SHOCK & AWE

Is your life messy or miraculous? Come on now and tell the truth.

Sadly, most of us feel like walking messes. Life has taken its toll on us, and we feel bloodied and beaten. But the Good News is that we don't have to stay that way.

From pastors to prisoners to saints and sinners, all of us need the unseen God unveiled before our eyes. It's here that a radical encounter with God Almighty can transform us forever. And if we're Christians, these encounters can happen *daily*.

I believe God desires to teach us how to sit down, be still, and look up.

I was reminded of this recently in my travels to Africa, among throngs of orphans.

For the last seven years our family traveled to Zambia, Africa, with a group called Family Legacy Missions International. Our family has helped to build a safe living place for the most vulnerable and destitute of children. While I was there something dawned on me.

One Sunday morning they led us in the most moving worship service through singing and prayers. I was struck by how much light resonates from their presence, and the profound faith in Jesus they profess.

Many of these children were raped, beaten, verbally abused, and left to themselves in poverty-stricken slums because their parents and caretakers died. Some even have HIV. But they're the most joyful, happy, friendly, and purposeful kids on this planet. They are crazy about their God because they understand He is crazy about them. These kids understand what it means to receive God's mercy, God's grace, and God's forgiveness. I must say, these children have a deep understanding of the presence of God.

As I watched them worship that day I kept thinking to myself, *What if these children kept their eyes on where they've come from? Instead of the wonderful life Jesus has called them to? How odd it would be!*

Yet, in American Christianity, isn't this what many of us do?

We focus on ourselves, we focus on our problems, we focus on our pasts, we focus on our fears, we focus on our failures, we focus, focus, focus, on everything but Christ.

Then, we wonder why our faith isn't working. And why we're such a mess.

Our eyes are fixed on the wrong things!

Somewhere we quit beholding Jesus. It's time to look back up!

Have you noticed how challenging it sometimes is to walk with God? When you *really* start to seek Him?

Why is this so?

That's a great question.

The reason is we live among intense spiritual warfare and don't even know it.

All that talk about a devil? *It's true.*

Because messages of spiritual warfare often get extremely complicated and oftentimes outright weird, many Christians shy away from the subject altogether.

But if we're going to be people who really have a handle on the Good News of Jesus, then we must consider the larger context in which you and I live. And the truth is, we cannot read through the New Testament without running into the topic of spiritual kingdoms, spiritual forces, principalities, powers, demons, deception, and spiritual battle imagery all over the place.

Nor can we disregard the fact that God is a supernatural being.

But here's what we do. We often unknowingly filter what we think about God through natural eyes, thus fitting God into a context we can grasp. We do this in an effort to wrap our brains around what we can't fully understand, the infinite and boundless mysteries of God.

So what I'm going to ask you to do is, pull back your lens by taking a moment to see the larger context of biblical understanding—with a kingdom mentality.

It's actually not hard when the Duchess of Cambridge from the British monarchy graces the covers of magazines, and the news media keeps us attuned to her happenings. Although the Royal Family lacks any real power in their monarchy, they help us contextualize a kingdom mentality.

I certainly don't want to scare you with this kind of talk, but you and I were born into the midst of two kingdoms at war: the kingdom of God and the kingdom of Satan. To be honest, the reality of this supernatural war of kingdoms surrounds us everywhere.

For instance, have you noticed how most narratives are laced with a good versus evil thread and thought to yourself, *Why is this so?* Or have you ever been bummed at the end of a movie when the story lacked a redemptive ending? Isn't good supposed to triumph over evil?

Or how about this one: What would you say gives a story that special "umpf"?

Wouldn't you agree the umpf is conflict?

Though we may not see it, there is a grander reality at work.

In the midst of a cosmic battle being waged, God's grand story has a redemptive end.

The good guy, who is King Jesus, really does win. Satan may have introduced some conflict, but make no mistake. His power is limited. He's a defeated foe.

But until God hurls him into his final destination, he ever lives to wreak havoc.

Where, you may ask? Here on planet Earth.

Let's take in these words from Revelation 12:12 with a fresh sense of sobriety:

> Woe to the earth and the sea, for the Devil has come
> down to you with great fury, because he knows he
> has a short time.

Satan's forte is killing, stealing, and destroying. And *we* are his targets in the middle of this supernatural unseen war zone. There's a real power of darkness at work.

Satan's number-one goal is to keep you in the darkness of your own sin. So highly distracted that you never look up to your Creator who longs to know you.

Whether that's through difficult people, difficult circumstances, or difficult upbringings, Satan's aim is to keep you feeling like a mess without any hope whatsoever and enmeshed in a steady stream of problems so you never reach out for God.

If he can't get you this way, he'll try to trick you into being your own god.

You don't need a Savior. *That's for weak people who need a crutch, right?*

And you'll never become *that* person! Sound familiar?

Yeah, I know his game. I've been there and done that.

Thankfully, Satan isn't getting the final word in your life. For God has said,

The Son of God was revealed for this purpose: to destroy the Devil's works. (1 John 3:8)

"If anyone enters by me, he will be saved and will go in and out and find pasture. The thief comes only to steal and kill and destroy. I came that they may have life and have it abundantly." (John 10:9–10 ESV)

I cannot beg you enough to choose Jesus' abundant life and live!

It's what you're dying for, thirsting for, hungering for, feverishly longing for, I promise! I know this from personal experience. Nothing, nothing, nothing does for us what Jesus wants to do for us. But we must take His hand and allow Him all ownership.

Previously I mentioned a huge element at stake in this kingdom war.

Would you like to know what this is besides each of our eternal destinies?

It's *worship*.

Satan will do anything to steal worship from God, directly or indirectly.

Did you know Satan exalts himself anytime someone rejects God?

Or when people worship false religions?

Or when they dabble in demonic activity such as reading horoscopes?

Or when communicators of God's Word preach a lesser gospel?

Honestly, he is worshipped by people living less than what God's Word says.

Truly, each of our lives is summed up by *worship*.

Can I ask you a probing question? *Is Satan being worshipped in your life?*

One way Satan usurps God's worship is when we become more self-aware than God-aware. What we're suffering from is a case of egotism, and we don't even know it. What I mean by egotism is loads of "us" on the brain. Can you relate? We can do this in negative and positive ways. A few examples might be obsessing over insecurities, talking about ourselves too much, nursing our wounds, flaunting our successes, name-dropping, and judging.

What's happened is our gaze has turned *inward*.

It's actually a version of self-infatuation. And we're eaten alive with it.

What I've been reminded of lately is true faith begins and ends with God as the grand subject. Transformation out of any mess only comes when we fix our eyes on Christ. This happens when we take Jesus' hand of help, and when we give Him the freedom to yank us out of the pit of self-consumption.

What we need to overcome is the staggering reality that we are not God.

Picking ourselves apart doesn't actually bring freedom from slavery of sin.

It enslaves us all the more. How so? We're suffocated by our powerlessness.

More than anything, this is why we're desperate for daily encounters.

In Scripture, when God shows up on the scene, most people fall on their faces, unless they're brazen and hard-hearted. Or they're entirely blinded by Satan and the scales on their eyes are thick. Which was my own story. It took repeated times of hearing the proclamation of Jesus, as well as experiencing God's presence, before I surrendered.

This was my husband's experience too.

In fact, my husband had an encounter recently, and it did him in.

With his permission, I'd like to share his story.

I had been teaching the Gospel of Luke for a good long while and I was *really moved* by all God was showing me through Luke's narrative. Few learning experiences compare to that of a teacher from being immersed in studying the Bible weekly. To be honest, I've taught plenty of other things—books of the Bible, topical series, short studies, long studies—but none had wrecked me like studying the book of Luke. I felt like my faith was forced to the utter edge.

How come, you ask?

My life and studies didn't match. Neither did some of my classes' participants.

I felt like a hypocrite. And I hate hypocrisy, *especially in myself.*

So as I taught through Luke and realized my life was not matching the call of Scripture, I knew I had two options: surrender or disobedience. I feared God too much not to choose surrender, and I called my class to join me by surrendering their lives too.

Here are some of the questions we pondered together:

- *Will we follow the God we say we love with absolute abandon?*
- *Or will we simply play church?*
- *Will we genuinely live as His people, withholding nothing?*
- *Or will we continue to live on in our spiritual mediocrity?*

All I can say is, God showed up and showed off each and every week!

As we threw open the living and active Word of God together, the presence of God would fill our room in a heavy weight of glory. There were times when I taught that I'd notice my hands trembling. It seemed as if the words from the pages of Scripture were springing to life right there in our Sunday school class when it says, "I will look favorably on this kind of person: one who is humble, submissive in spirit, and trembles at My word" (Isa. 66:2). I was trembling all right.

God was in our midst and we happily fell under the authority of God in prayer, and begged Him to do what He was teaching us through His Word, *in us.*

Sometimes I encountered God so powerfully at home while studying the Scriptures, I couldn't speak. Other times the weight of God's glory would rest on me so heavy that all I could do was sit there and weep for His nearness, His goodness, and His unfailing love. Then, Lord help me, there were other times I just could not shut up.

This happens to us teacher kinds. We struggle to keep to ourselves the sweetness of what we're learning. It feels like a balloon needing to be popped. But not everybody wants a lesson or deep theological talk. And sometimes we don't care whether you want it or not 'cause we know you *need* it. Or at least we think you do anyway. Sometimes we need to stuff a sock in it, like the night Erin nonchalantly asked me what I was studying. When he gave me *the* look, I knew something was wrong. So I tried to tiptoe back gently.

Perhaps I should explain.

I had been studying all day the life of Christ's most prominent disciples, particularly their lives *after* Jesus' resurrection and ascension back into heaven, when the Holy Spirit of God came to live *within* them. I was all fired up for what I was seeing.

Before long Erin was due home, so I called it a day and shut the books.

Within no time, Erin came happily through the door. And, like usual, we sat at the breakfast table for a bit and downloaded our day. When he asked how my day was and what I was studying, I got so fired up I nearly knocked him out with my flood of passion.

"You know, honey, I've been looking at the lives of the disciples . . . how they *tore up* the earth for the kingdom of God. I'm so stunned by how we have *God* living on the inside of us but live *so* casual to His presence. Like it's no big deal! I just don't understand how we can call ourselves Christ followers but live such mediocre lives. What in the world is our problem?"

When he crossed his arms and glared at me I knew he was ticked.

Uh-oh. I had obviously struck a nerve or something.

So I tried to tiptoe back a few notches and asked nicely, "Honey, what's wrong?"

That's when he replied: "I'm not going to tell you because you'll get mad."

"No, I really do want you to tell me. I want to know."

Because now he had me downright curious. Seeing how this was hitting him piqued my interest, actually. And suddenly I said, "Hold that thought!" Not only did I want to hear what he had to say, I also wanted to be sure and write it all down. His wrestlings are precious treasures to his woman—I like hearing how he's working it out.

This is what he had to say (just as I wrote it down that day) concerning the following questions:

Why do we live such mediocre lives when we have God living in us?

What in the world is our problem?

- I'm too comfortable where I'm at.
- Too afraid to step out because of failure that could happen.
- I feel like I live under the Enemy's thumb—right where he wants me.

In hindsight, I wish I hadn't been so blinded by zeal in the moment. I should've tempered it with a little more graciousness since I knew my husband grappled at times with spiritual mediocrity a little more than me and, sadly, the mediocrity sometimes won.

But, to be honest, it did not cross my mind until afterward.

Now this is a man who attends church regularly, and has for years. He goes on mission trips to Africa, and not only ministers to orphans but also loves them deeply. He listens to podcast messages often from some of the foremost leading preachers around. And not only does he read his Bible nearly every day but he's also a man of prayer. But sometimes—in all of his doings—he struggles with handing over his heart *fully*.

Want to hear something wild?

God ripped the rug right out from under Erin's feet after that talk.

After that conversation, Erin went into a time of deep depression. At first, I didn't know what was happening, and I was scared to death. But then the Lord clued me in. God was working in Erin's life to force a holy desperation.

And it worked.

His mediocrity is gone. His list is gone. These days Erin Head is *fully* His.

Radical encounters with God often happen like this. The ground starts quaking. And our reasons for living come crashing down. Our motivations are exposed. And we're left naked and defenseless before a holy God. The holiness of God has stripped us bare.

But we're certainly not meant to stay devastated.

The ongoing plan of God is to build us into sincere lovers of Him who live elated and enlivened by His presence day after day. But having our spiritual eyes blown open by the Lord God Almighty is *highly necessary*, and comes first and foremost in our ability to attain more of God.

This kind of encounter actually happened to a man named Isaiah.

Let's look at his story now.

In the year that King Uzziah died, I saw the Lord seated on a high and lofty throne, and His robe filled the temple. Seraphim were standing above Him; each one had six wings: with two he covered his face, with two he covered his feet, and with two he flew. And one called to another:

Holy, holy, holy is the LORD of Hosts; His glory fills the whole earth.

The foundations of the doorways shook at the sound of their voices, and the temple was filled with smoke.

Then I said:

Woe is me for I am ruined because I am a man of unclean lips and live among a people of unclean lips, and because my eyes have seen the King, the LORD of Hosts.

Then one of the seraphim flew to me, and in his hand was a glowing coal that he had taken from the altar with tongs. He touched my mouth with it and said: Now that this has touched your lips, your wickedness is removed and your sin is atoned for. Then I heard the voice of the Lord saying: Who should I send? Who will go for Us? I said: Here I am. Send me. (Isa. 6:1–8)

Notice the progression of Isaiah's encounter with God.

First, he sees God elevated in majesty, occupying a throne of worship. There's no question the Almighty is something to behold. The sheer responsive praise of the angels is nothing short of dramatic. God's presence captivates everybody's attention. The angels are awestruck of the One they see night and day from eternity past up to eternity present. They cannot get over how unmistakably amazing their Creator is.

Next, our gaze shifts to Isaiah's response, and he's undeniably slain. The God Isaiah was beholding is far too grand for his fleshly humanity to stand. Instantly he's undone before this holy God. There's no need to convince Isaiah of his sin. A mere moment in the Lord's presence uncovered his wretchedness. One thing was certain: he and his God are *nothing* at all alike, obviously. But the story doesn't end there. And aren't we glad?

Then, we behold God's graciousness. Once Isaiah confessed his sin, the angel came to purify his mouth, using a hot coal taken from the altar of God. God's forgiveness and grace are poured out upon Isaiah's life, and he can now stand securely in the presence of his holy God. Isaiah sees that his God is not only majestic in glory but also compassionate and kind. And he is wasted for this wonderful God of grace.

Lastly, Isaiah's knees buckle and his hands lift. For when his Lord questioned, *"Who should I send? Who will go for Me?"* Isaiah had nothing to say other than, "Here I am. Send me." Basically Isaiah was saying, "Whatever, Lord. I am Yours entirely."

Have you encountered God's presence in a profound way?

If not, consider saying this prayer to God now.

Father, I give myself to You now. Would You fling open my eyes to the majestic glory of Your presence? Shock me, scare me, and startle me in a way that my only response will be to unreservedly bow myself before You.

We can apply a few things to our own lives from Isaiah's encounter with God.

Any significant change in our life begins with encountering God first. "At the heart of the Christian message is God Himself waiting for His redeemed children to push in to conscious awareness of His presence."[3] *To push in to.* Tozer's use of words are highly fitting for us. Would you agree one reason we struggle to engage God's presence is because of the effort it takes? I think so. Our spirit is willing but our flesh is weak, and our flesh often wins the fight since it's highly spoiled and demanding.

I bet if we did some investigative work we'd quickly iden-
tify that many of our spiritual predicaments are attributed to
our laziness to seek after and sit with God.

Truth be told, we have a two-faced human dwelling
inside of us.

Our spirit wants God to show up mightily in our lives.
It longs to find release, and to run with God unhindered. It
hungers for more of God's Spirit, for more of His abiding
with us. But the fleshly sinful nature part of us? It resists the
holiness of God, and runs away. It doesn't like the boundaries the holiness of God requires. In fact, this is the side of us
that often talks us out of yielding to God because it highly
resents submission to God's authority.

But to refuse God's presence is to throw open the doors
of our life to destruction. We might think our choice to rebel
against God's authority is freedom—as if we're blazing a trail
of our own confident strength and independence. Little do
we know, rebellion to the authority of God will not fare well
for us. We think we're running to freedom when, actually,
we're running into a deeper abyss of dark spiritual wreckage.

Interestingly, right after Isaiah unreservedly declared to
God, "Here I am. Send me," God sent Isaiah forth on a mission to speak to a people who were lifeless to God.

Hear the word of the Lord for these ones through His
prophet:

> He said, "Go and tell this people:
> 'Listen hard, but you aren't going to get it;
> look hard, but you won't catch on.'
> Make these people blockheads,
> with fingers in their ears and blindfolds on their eyes,
> So they won't see a thing,
> won't hear a word,
> So they won't have a clue about what's going on
> and, yes, so they won't turn around and be made
> whole." (Isa. 6:9–10 MSG)

Did you catch the intent of God in the last sentence?

What He longs to do for people, even when He knows these people won't accept?

Our God wants to make us *whole.*

And this is Who we refuse?

What freedom we'd find if we woke up from our slumber and turned back around.

ᥱᷱ

I must confess, I'm saddened for the masses of people who reject God's grace and, sadly, never receive what He was so ready to give them had they yielded to Him.

If only they had looked up. If only they had cried out. If only they had humbled themselves by acknowledging God's realness, God's lordship, and God's gift of eternal life through Jesus' life, death, burial, and resurrection.

But this kind of giving up of personal control scares folks.

So does owning up to our sinfulness—especially if we've lived as "good" people.

However, to receive the fullness of intimacy the Lord desires to bestow on us, we must believe in the serious reasons for Jesus Christ to die on the cross, which was to pardon all of us from our sins. When Jesus—the sinless Savior—bore our sin, He paid the penalty of sin for us, in our place. God's judgment toward sin is eternal death but, in Christ, by faith in His saving grace, we are saved from God's judgment of sin.

As we give our life to Jesus, He gives Himself to us. His life envelops ours, and when the Holy One looks our way He sees the debt is paid. By receiving Jesus Christ as Lord, we are God's and God is ours. The Father of all Creation has lovingly and happily adopted us for His very own—for eternity forevermore.

When we encounter God, His presence awakens us to new life. Just like Isaiah, when the Spirit of God throws back our eyelids to His presence and we surrender our lives to His lordship, *everything* changes. We are spiritually reborn. New birth is vital since Jesus said, "I tell you the truth, no one can enter the kingdom of God unless he is born of water and the Spirit. Flesh gives birth to flesh, but the Spirit gives birth to spirit. . . . 'You must be born again'" (John 3:5–7 NIV).

The beauty of spiritual rebirth is not only does God become our Father but also our Father's life comes to life in us through the indwelling of the Holy Spirit. New birth in the Spirit not only flings heaven's gates open wide when we die but also heaven's life is imparted to us as we continue to live. This is the wonder of spiritual regeneration. As the Spirit works in us, our "spiritual senses" are brought forth to life by *God's life.*

Thus, to walk with God is to live in step with His life every day.

This is worthy of consideration because our five senses (taste, touch, smell, hearing, sight) are our means for interpreting data in journeying through life. Our five senses are highly necessary for discerning correctly, and making proper decisions accordingly. Without our senses we would live numbed to life. Our senses help to animate us, to empower us and, interestingly, to also individualize us.

It is true for our spiritual senses as well. We need the Spirit to awaken our senses. So we can see the Spirit, hear the Spirit, engage with the Spirit, understand the Spirit, and know the Spirit. This awakening happens in the presence of God and through repentance.

If we want more of God, we cannot remain spiritual wimps by sidestepping or shrinking back on honest confession before God. Like Isaiah, we must tremble before the holiness of God and cry out, "Woe is me." We must do the work of personal confession of sin, just like Isaiah did.

For one, we must confront our personal responsibility for our spiritual lethargy. We've allowed ourselves the room to have a happy heyday, spiritually sabotaging ourselves for far too long. Indeed the carnal side of our humanity has lived a spoiled brat lifestyle by living a highly undisciplined life.

Second, we must confront our personal responsibility of allowing Satan the room to have a happy heyday, by giving him plenty of our cooperation to work with for too long.

I must warn you, though. Fully engaging with God requires our true self to come forth. This can be painful because our true self often lives in denial of being truthful to itself. As we move into the light, the holiness of God exposes our inner darkness. To go higher is to go lower in God's economy. For in the Father's presence is found awe and wonder, *yes*. But holiness and truth are as much a part of His person as His unfailing love.

For those of us who are brave enough to call the shots as God sees them and not as we see them, the holiness and truth of God beckons us to bow down in repentance and surrender. Confess any and all areas of sin, own up to any and all areas of needed transformation, and give God the room to heal what He wants to and to transform what He wants to—no qualms.

I hate to be so serious, but you and I have got to wake up from our slumber.

We need a fresh encounter where we're rattled to the core, like Isaiah. The presence of God ushered forth a dazzling elation to Isaiah's senses and a devastating need for repentance to Isaiah's senses too. Like Isaiah, God awakens our senses and it shakes us to the core entirely. Interestingly, the elation we feel in God's presence dazzles us by drawing us near, while the devastation we feel in God's presence provokes us to repent so we can abide in His presence. Holiness is necessary since "without it no one will see the Lord" (Heb. 12:14).

Being ruined is key to finding more of God and walking in the vitality of His Spirit, where we're slain by His majesty, and holiness, and realness, and otherworldliness. So much so, we're "scared" into a spiritually correct frame of our mind. Truth is, we've forgotten whom it is we're dealing with. Some of us have taken on a mind-set like Peyton when she was little. I'll never forget the time we picked her up from summer camp when she was around nine years old, and we asked her what she learned.

"I learned God isn't just a big grandpa in the sky."

Shock and awe. I knew exactly what she meant.

Peyton has been blessed to have *the sweetest* granddaddy in the world. The two are tight. His little "Peytie" (as he affectionately calls her) can do no wrong. His nine-year-old granddaughter and her darling set of dimples did a number on him. She had him wrapped.

What she learned at camp was this: "God isn't exactly like Pop."

No, Darling. He's not.

When God Almighty unveils His true self before our eyes, it scares us to death. And it should! This is God we're dealing with—majestic and holy, none can compare.

WE MUST FLING WIDE-OPEN THE DOORS OF OUR HEARTS & INVITE THE Light OF God's loving Presence INTO EVERY NOOK AND CRANNY.

#MORE

chapter four

letting LOVE in

Awakening to the freedom found in God's presence can *revolutionize* a life.

Running into a ramshackle soul can change the course of book plans too.

I wasn't planning on writing this particular book. I had another one in mind, a marriage book. Not that I'm an expert wife or anything. Nothing could be further from the truth. I just had an itch to encourage married women.

But my plans of writing a marriage book took a radical turn one day after I walked into a tiny boutique and encountered a woman. I wasn't planning on going there. But my doctor's appointment wrapped up early leaving me with some time to kill. I had only been to the store once or twice. What I remembered most was the owner. She was a beautiful South American woman, in her late fifties.

For some odd reason, I wanted to tell her so.

I kept thinking, *What woman dislikes hearing she's beautiful?*

So I waited until the time was right.

When she handed me my purchases, I looked in her eyes and said, "You are the most beautiful woman. What in the world are you doing? Whatever it is, it's working!" The words hardly escaped my lips when she fell completely apart.

"Oh, honey. Thank you. If you only knew the things going on in my life! Well, you wouldn't say that to me. I have so much hurt inside. When I look in the mirror I think to myself, *Look at you. You are a mess.* My husband recently left me after thirty years of marriage for a younger woman. I've spent years maintaining myself . . . for what?" With tears streaming down her face she said, "In ten years I'll be seventy! Then what? How could God allow me to go through such pain? What am I to do with my life now? My business is terrible. My son is upset with me. I'm losing my home. I'm losing my financial security. How on earth will I take care of myself now?"

Man. Her hopelessness and pain felt awfully familiar.

Suddenly, I had second thoughts about that marriage book.

That's when I realized *that* message would stand to be salt in this woman's wounds. Sure she could believe God and pray for restoration—but she needed serious hope for her own brokenness and comfort for her soul.

I was so perplexed by her pain I rambled off something stupid: "I'm actually writing a marriage book."

When she replied, "Darling, will it help me? I'll read it if it'll help me!"

All I could say was, "I'm so sorry, but I don't think it will."

Then my mind drifted off for a few seconds. . . . I wanted so much to put a resource in her hands that would speak to her heart and bring healing to her bones. Something she could read when her nights lasted forever and her mind wouldn't shut off and her body couldn't sleep—something on how Jesus Christ could change her life forever. Being a lover of books—so many have helped me—I deeply longed to give her one.

Thankfully, I snapped back to reality to love on her a little.

But I couldn't get away from thinking how different her life could be if she really, I mean *really*, encountered God, and experienced His redeeming love found in Jesus Christ.

That's when I decided to get bold.

"Did you know your latter years with God can be better than all of your former years combined?" With tear-stained cheeks she blinked her eyes and nodded her head a little; I'm uncertain she believed me. But I know it's the truth since I'm a woman who's experienced it firsthand. I wanted so much to tell her my story, for her to hear how my latter years with God have far outweighed my former years without Him. God has so redeemed my life from utter darkness—it's a wild story of redemption—if only she would look to Him!

But she had other customers to tend to by now, and time didn't allow.

I left so burdened for her pain I could hardly stand it.

I prayed for her for days. I begged God to transform her by making her life into a miracle. Then my stomach soured over that marriage book altogether.

Interestingly, days later, God spoke to my heart.

He said He didn't just take messy *marriages* and turn them into walking miracles. He takes messy *people* and turns them into walking miracles. He hasn't just done a wonder in my marriage. He's done a wonder in my soul. I am a walking miracle of God. That's what He wanted me to write about. He wanted me to tell others how they, too, can become walking miracles of God.

It's interesting how encounters can change the course of your life in an instant. We can be minding our own business when all of a sudden, *bam*, everything changes. That's what happened to me when I walked into that tiny boutique and encountered her. It's also what happened to me the day I encountered Jesus. Like that beautiful woman, I was a mess with no hope whatsoever. But God not only rescued me, He's liberating me.

I wonder if He's doing the same for you? Pursuing you? Longing to liberate you? I'm not just talking about liberating you in the sense of changing the course of your eternal destiny. I'm talking about having a living and active relationship with God where He is personally involved in your day-to-day affairs—so much so—that you live in a supernatural fullness of His ongoing liberating presence.

That's what becoming a walking miracle looks like. Where the life you're living in Christ is such a far cry from the life you would be living without Him. What I'm talking about is a life that walks in the supernatural power and presence of God *daily*. A life not bound by the fallen nature anymore—a life on an adventure with God.

We were made for more.

You know this is why Jesus came?

Your life means more to Him than you think.

If you throw open the Bible and bury your nose in it you'll discover this.

The Bible is not just another book. It's the redemptive plan of God.

There's something said for laying it open and reading the whole thing.

You'll soon discover what the Gospel of Luke states is very true: "For the Son of Man has come to seek and to save the lost" (Luke 19:10).

⟡

My family actually committed to the faithful jaunt of reading the entire Bible together in a year. We'd each read the same selections from a chronological Bible. I'm laughing now. Erin was the sole survivor. The other three of us fell out at different times, but I assure you I *did* observe some recognizable truths: We are a messy people. God is a patient God. All of us desperately need Him. And He longs to liberate us.

Not only did Erin read the entire Bible in a year, he did it again. And it changed him. Like I said, there's something said for laying the book open and discovering God's redemptive plan for ourselves.

Seeing God seek.
Seeing God liberate.
Seeing God so determined about it too.

If you stick with your readings, when you get to the New Testament, particularly Luke 4:16–21, your heart begins stirring with emotion. God came to earth, in the form of a man, Jesus of Nazareth, *finally* here to save us.

Let's look at the verses together:

> When he came to the village of Nazareth, his boyhood home, he went as usual to the synagogue on the Sabbath and stood up to read the Scriptures. The scroll of Isaiah the prophet was handed to him. He unrolled the scroll and found the place where this was written: "The Spirit of the LORD is upon me, for he has anointed me to bring Good News to the poor. He has sent me to proclaim that captives will be released, that the blind will see, that the oppressed will be set free, and that the time of the LORD's favor has come." He rolled up the scroll, handed it back to the attendant, and sat down. All eyes in the synagogue looked at him intently. Then he began to speak to them. "The Scripture you've just heard has been fulfilled this very day!" (Luke 4:16–21 NLT)

This can be fulfilled in your life today too.

Are you feeling captive in areas? Blind in areas? Oppressed in areas?

Hear this good news personally today: *Jesus releases people from walking messes to walking miracles.*

Some religious voices today don't paint this picture of God and it makes me sad. To them God requires, and expects, and hard-drives with a fastidious scowl on His face matching an angry, corrective tone to His voice. When they speak of the Bible, it's through the lilt of do and do, be and be. But this isn't all of God. That's only *half* of Him. Sure, He's definitely a God who rightly judges sin—a God of the

Holy Law. And without a doubt He's fierce and holy and demands obedience. But this isn't a full disclosure of God. Truth is, God satisfied His own righteous requirements by taking on human flesh as a tiny babe, lying in a manger. He then grew up to die a criminal's death on our behalf in order to provide us welcoming intimacy through Jesus.

Perhaps baby Jesus to them is Christmas nostalgia? I'm unsure. But to me, from what I've discovered all over the Bible, Jesus is God's grace gift revealed *to* us and given *for* us—if we'll receive Him—who has come to set our captive hearts free from eternal destruction, depravity, and dead-end living.

Jesus came to give us God's abundant life, a relationship unlike any other—a relationship consisting of deepest love, amazing redemption, and one with a crazy promise: *With Me you can live a triumphant life, a life you've never dreamed. All because I live in you.* Jesus gives us the ability to walk and talk and live as free people—enjoying God forever.

How so?

Because in Jesus' sinless body sacrificed on Calvary's cross—the sinless, spotless Lamb—satisfied God's wrath against sin. This is wonderful and glorious Good News for you and me! You and I don't have to measure up to a holy God. Christ did this for us.

Oh, man, to even think on it now stirs deepest emotions.

(And if you're tempted to think, *Oh, I've been a Christian for years, I know all about the cross, I don't need to hear this again,* I beg you to bear with me, friend. The Good News of what Christ did on the cross never gets old and is always worth telling and hearing again and again.)

To be honest, I wish I had surrendered my life to Christ sooner.

I was so clueless to what I was resisting, such a glorious, loving, forgiving God.

Are you clueless right now too?

I want you to know, the same Savior who walked into a synagogue two thousand years ago and openly declared He was the One sent "to proclaim that captives will be released, that the blind will see, that the oppressed will be set free, and that the time of the LORD's favor has come," hasn't ended His mission.

He's still seeking. He's still liberating. He's still determined.

Our problem is, we struggle connecting with Him long enough to receive it.

God wants to teach us in a greater way how to crawl up into His arms of love.

You're not the only one with trust issues.

I'd venture to say we all have areas of struggling to trust a God we can't see.

Just throw a tragic situation or painful circumstance our way and hear what spews:

God, why did You allow this to happen?
God, why didn't You do something? You could have.
God, do You care? Do You see how much we're hurting?

Those are questions stemming from the waters of distrust.

I was reminded of this not long ago in my own life.

Truth is, beneath our heaps of junk, and mess, and confusion is a sense of desperation. I'm seeing it everywhere I turn. People everywhere are desperate for something *more*. We're broken. We're beaten up. And many of us are thinking to ourselves, *Wasn't life supposed to be better than this?*

I assure you, I'm not taking a guess at this. I actually asked my hairdresser about it one day. I needed to know from someone with a front row seat into people's lives if she was seeing what I'm seeing, that something alarming is taking place. People are seriously hurting. Barely limping along. Grappling in darkness. Outright overcome.

"Girl, would you say people seem uncharacteristically messy? Going through really hard times? Unable to catch their breath? Really beaten down?" I asked.

"Absolutely. You wouldn't even believe it."

"Hmm . . . that's what I thought."

Here are a few stories I know firsthand:

- One family is fighting for the heart of their daughter. She was seduced into an abusive relationship by someone they trusted. How did this happen? And will they ever fully heal?
- Another family is doing their best to pick up the pieces, and to heal, after their son tragically committed suicide. God is carrying them through. *But why God, why?*
- There's a beautiful, bright, and godly young woman who has lost her way. Not only is she addicted to drugs, homeless, and confused—but to deny her God too?
- A husband tragically died in front of his wife while vacationing together. What a devastating tragedy and loss. But she was hardly able to mourn because her parents suddenly fell terribly ill with cancer. *Lord, is this pain not way too much?*
- A teen girl is in trouble *again*. This time her family isn't handling it so well. They've spiraled into an exceedingly dark place. In their fears they've gotten angry—now they're struggling with shameful regrets. Will they ever rebuild their lives after this kind of devastation? This isn't at all what they've prayed for, hoped for, worked toward as they've raised her.
- One wife just found a suggestive text message on her husband's phone. She's trying so hard to forgive and make this marriage work. But anger and fear and doubt keep resurrecting itself in her heart. Questions plague her mind. *Have I really forgiven? Will I ever*

be a loving, trusting wife again? Will I ever fully recover? She hopes so, but she's emotionally unsure. She's a strong woman, but this nearly has her completely beat.

- Then there's a thirty-something single woman who wonders if she's just "messed up." Why hasn't a man taken interest in her? Is something inherently wrong? Is she even worthy of love? She reaffirms her hope constantly. She knows her identity isn't wrapped up in a man. But the battle for her confidence is fierce.

- There's another couple I know who has lost everything. And I do mean *everything*. Their fortunes crashed with the economy. They lost their home, their cars, their upstanding reputations in their community, and *all* of their material possessions. To make matters worse, even their kids have turned against them—eaten alive with bitterness and resentment at their parents for losing it all. Will they ever recover from such devastating loss?

Or *me*. The one writing this book. Truth is, I sat in my hairdresser's chair that day emotionally limping along myself. Trying to wear a happy face without crying or worse—wearing her out from a stream of pitiful complaints. But I wasn't just asking my question with a curiosity for others. I was asking it with a curiosity for myself. Deep down I needed to know from someone else's perspective: Are you seeing this too? Am I alone? Are others feeling this same way? Am I just crazy? Or is *something* overtly desperate happening? Though I hate knowing others are feeling this same way, I was dually relieved by her reply.

I think I even said to her, "So, I'm not crazy after all?"

Frankly, I'm not just a woman well acquainted with messes. I'm a woman well acquainted with how to get out of one too. Having walked with God for years now, I know the steps to living a victorious life in Christ. I've not just tasted and seen that the Lord is good. I've lived in God's presence finding boundless freedom and ecstatic joy.

Nevertheless, within days of formulating this book into a proposal, all hell broke loose in my household—and I do mean literally. For instance, my handsome husband slipped into a sudden and serious state of depression. At times, I feared he would end his life because of sheer hopelessness. We've been married for years, and this wasn't the strong man I had come to love and do life with. Obviously we took our vows with truckloads of personal baggage in tow. But depression was never his issue. Maybe mine, but certainly not his.

Then, both of our daughters were simultaneously thrown for ugly loops—each battling hard and hurtful situations. There's nothing quite like being a mother and watching your children dwell in messes you can't snatch them out of or control.

For a while, I was strong and secure. Then I lost my footing and landed in the worst place spiritually and emotionally since becoming a Christian. When I say darkness eclipsed my entire person I am not even kidding. I couldn't pray. I couldn't read my Bible. I couldn't sleep without medicine. Nightmares seized my nights. Fears seized my days. Tears became my food and drink—my very best friends. I couldn't get my act together for anything and, quite honestly, I quit trying.

Utter brokenness of my soul engulfed me.

Then to ice this ugly awful cake—for months on end— my mind experienced an onslaught of doubts over *everything* I'd believed about God thus far. I asked questions I never (and I do mean never!) thought I would ask. Questions like:

- Is God even real?
- Is Christianity really true?
- Are we all believing a bunch of nonsense?

I have no problem with people asking questions like these. But when you've known God to the degree that I've known

Him—this was altogether *strange*. Some would suggest it's good I asked these questions—especially in an increasingly post-modern, post-Christian time in our nation—but for me this was a place of deepest suffering.

I haven't just known God—I've *known* God. He's more real to me than what my eyes can see and what my mind can conceive. I don't just know Him. *I know that I know that I know Him.*

Not only did I encounter God's presence powerfully in my early twenties. But I've had other encounters with God's presence, causing me to fall prostrate before Him in reverential fear.

I've observed visible transformations of people going from darkness to light—so extraordinary—my only response was to love God all the more. I've beheld God's power so demonstrative. I've experienced His holiness so chilling. And I've found the Holy Scriptures not as simple words on a page—they are active, living words jumping off simple pages, taking on resurrection life in those who read and believe.

The Holy Scriptures have been life to my dead bones— giving vision, clarity, and equipping me for life and godliness. God has used them so specifically and miraculously to heal my body. God has used them so specifically and miraculously to heal my broken mind. God has used them so specifically and miraculously to give words to prayers so private they were only whispers from within—then He answered them.

You better believe, I've watched God defy all odds with my life. I've watched God defy all odds with my marriage. I promise you, I am in no way just a good person, or a determined woman who finally learned how to make a few good decisions in her life. I am a living, breathing, nothing-short-of-miraculous, walking miracle of God.

This is the reason my heart was so wrenched by those overwhelming doubts.

You don't have to tell me He's real. I *know* He's real.

So, if you're feeling like a mess right now, be encouraged.
I get it.

I can also assure you that masses alongside you are going
through similar difficulties. You're not crazy—thinking
times are hard. They are. You're not just a wimp—unable to
handle things like you used to. The storms really are raging.
You're not just being a drama queen—emotionally losing
it for nothing. Something in the heavenly places is honestly shaking. Times really are changing. Something is up.
Someone is trying to fully get our attention. And I think it's
time we began listening, don't you?

❦

You and me—we were made for love.

Can we pick back up on the precious orphan girl I told
you about in chapter 1?

Like her, I was once lifeless yet breathing. Full of darkness, hollow eyes, wounded appendages, and severely dis-
trusting of anything wrapped in human flesh. Our only
difference was I grew up to play the game of pretense, the
game of pretend. Most hardly knew a stone wall miles thick
encompassed my heart.

Suddenly, God pricked my heart.

*All of you, you were made for love. When you don't get
it, it's devastating.*

This was not new news, but a staggering remembrance.
God knew my heart was hemorrhaging from one too many
stabs of suffering, my faith was drained dry. I had not been
this messy in years. Nor could I get my act together. Sheer
will, determination, survivorship, slapping on a happy
face—vanquished.

I sensed what He was saying; I could read between the
lines.

All of us run from what we need most—the love of God.

The grander the messiness, the grander the guarding it seems. Many, even us Christians, hardly know we were made for love. Nor do we let down our guarded hearts enough to sit in the arms of our gracious God so He can love us to life by proving His promise from John 10:10 is experientially true.

"I have come so that they may have life and have it in abundance."

In all honesty, sitting in God's presence holding that orphan, God undid me.

Her suffering stabbed my own heart afresh. Memories of my troubled life flooded my mind. Though I was reared in a family, I grew up feeling orphaned. God has healed my heart of so much pain. Yet days come when the sting of it all returns.

Around that time, my soul was aching for a momma to talk to. God has richly supplied me a momma in my mother-in-law. But this day I had a problem—her son.

All I can say is, don't mess with a woman's son, even if she does like you.

I am partly kidding. Barbara loves me enough to patiently listen.

But I also love her enough to carefully guard her heart from unnecessary worry.

Perhaps this wish for a momma was a constructed idol I had allowed to fester in my head. I won't deny the possibility. But in my wish for a perfect world, for things to be as they *ought* and not as they are, here is what I have believed a mother to be in this present season of my own life of wrestlings: Mothers are a masterpiece of beauty wrapped in the feminine warmth of fleshly colored skin tones. She lets you cry today, knowing you will rise up to the fight tomorrow. She graces your temporary need for insanity when you *really do not want to* perform well, or strike a robust pose of praiseworthy faith. She's safe . . . for after meltdowns good sense does return. So do laughter, cups of coffee, and warm chocolate chip cookies from her oven.

Okay, I'm throwing in a little romanticism there—but you get my drift?

I have a mom actually.

She's somewhere in my city though I have not seen her in a good long while. I grace her before God, praying for her often. I'm saddened my ancestry's beginnings were found in the wastelands of godless living from as far back as I know, or have heard. Our family fields for harvesting a good life were barren—generation after generation after generation. Any semblance of healthfulness was not our lot. We were poor, uneducated messes. Wind-sucking survivors always up for a rebellious fight.

Jerry Springer ain't got nothin' on us.

Honestly, the older I get, as do my beautiful girls, I shudder sometimes. Or sob. Why God handpicked me for Himself, I do not know. Other than maybe He would use my life in this hopeless generation to say, *Run to God! Give Him your life! He is the more you are longing for!*

I only have thoughts of love where my family is concerned. All bitterness of heart was dealt a deathblow many, many years ago. I hold no one in hostage in any form of unforgiveness. I say this because my hope is for you to allow God to take you there too. Truth is, I have been the worst of all sinners. God's grace on my life is nothing short of scandalous. To hold another in contempt would be sickening, actually.

I shall also never give up hope of us dancing on the beautiful streets of redemption together one day. Where tears are no more, where each is understood, where hearts have abundant freedom to flow freely back and forth because all is finally finished forevermore . . . However, I also must trust God to rest in His Sovereign plan of restoration.

But who knows? I do believe in a God of miracles. I welcome His works.

Honestly, entrusting these relationships into God's trustworthy hands was gruesome, but freeing. Not all relationships wrap up into gorgeous pretty bows. To say so is not lacking faith. For me, it's immeasurable liberty. The yokes of guilt have nearly killed all life in me. Long after God released me to walk on, wholly released.

In this world we are subjected to unhappy endings. But the glory of knowing God personally is we await the arrival of the happiest of beginnings that will never, ever end. All of eternity is a celebration of how we *knew* things should have been.

I welcome the day when heaven eclipses all painful memories finally, fully, and blessedly forevermore. I imagine if heaven has a field of wildflowers somewhere you may find me holding my momma's hand—running, leaping, acting like giggly girls—joyful, at peace, home free.

Until then, I set this mess before my God as an offering of trust and patience.

Listen, Jesus offers us a better way than hardening up and living as victims of our circumstances or taking a survivor's stance. But in order to live this kind of life in Christ, we must allow God to break our wounds afresh in His trustworthy hands. We must fling wide-open the doors of our hearts and invite the light of God's loving presence into every secret nook and cranny—bravely withholding nothing, exposing everything, where all secret places and spaces are welcome to His knowing, His forgiveness, and His cleansing.

The problem is, our culture has raised us to dress up in happy faces—*for a good performance is highly esteemed.* We applaud the strong and scorn the weak. We favor the rich and look down on the poor. We elevate the wise and learned and look down on the uneducated, the homeless, and the marginal strugglers of society. We raise up big girls and boys who buck up, and step up, and despise all signs of weakness, as ones who are approved. The majority of us are, therefore, only a more grown-up version of Baby C.

Our lack of trust shows it.

Our lack of attachment shows it.

Our isolation and loneliness and stone-walling show it.

But to heal we must let down, admit to our mess, and allow God to love us to life in Him. And this is scary. What we are afraid of is becoming undone. We think to ourselves, *What happens when we let down, allowing ourselves to be loved by a God we can't see or touch or even smell? Furthermore, what is life like devoid of pretense and pretending? Will we lose it? Will we somehow get better?*

Then quadruple the fear if your raising took place in a moralistic religious environment where godly performances mattered more than engaging the heart of God, being loved by Him, and loving Him back. If God was a distant heavenly acquaintance who was more like a sheriff instead of a loving daddy, you will certainly fight fears. You'll likely wonder, can God *really* be trusted? Will He have mercy on my frailties, or harshly rage against all of my faults? Will He leave me broken and shamed, or will He love, forgive, and promise to heal? What happens when I let Him in—*all the way in*?

Well, Baby C—a year later—is the happiest, most delightful, most darling little girl you have ever laid your eyes upon. Her eyes dance of light, her heart is full of love, and her appendages are no longer limp and lifeless. In the safety of the Tree of Life Children's Village, in the safety of the love of God, Baby C is abounding in energy, talking like crazy, giggling and laughing and happily scurrying about because Jesus is doing a supernatural, powerful healing in her formerly traumatized heart—using the hands and love and faithful work of her caretakers to be Him with skin on. The miraculous love of God is healing her—she's transforming exponentially.

I saw a picture taken of her just recently, and I wanted to bawl.

She's trusting! She's attaching! She's no longer bound in fearful soul isolation!

I'd say she's a walking miracle of God, wouldn't you?

And you can be one too.

As we draw this chapter to a close, I'd love to share something God spoke over my heart after holding the little orphans in my arms that day. Perhaps you need it too?

He always wanted you. Before you came to be. Before your beautiful limbs and life were delicately crafted in your mother's womb. You were pondered in His own heart and mind. Never were you a mistake or a complicated burden. You were His then. You are His now. And you will be His forevermore.

The words He speaks and sings and shouts over you are life, hope, peace, joy, and uniqueness in personality to bring Him much pleasure and your greatest good. Do not entertain lies today. This will only cause you to come into disagreement, confusion, fearfulness, frustration, and duress for not accepting what He says is true.

Did you know God has announced His love for you in the cosmos? Where angels and demons dwell? Indeed, He has eulogized you before these ones—you are His.

He has taken your every yoke onto His person, bearing it Himself. And He has exchanged your captivity for liberty—in heart, soul, mind, and strength—by Himself.

You need not worry. You need not fret. . . . Sit down. Be still. Look up.

He IS the One who satisfies you. He IS the One who approves you. He IS the One who releases you. The more you relax in His arms, the more you shall live and breathe, and be a source of Him to the world—the world where He has apportioned you to live and give away His life and love. Know this, child. You are His joy. You are His delight.

Relax, dear one. Be refreshed in His presence, and let His love in.

God IS RAISING US UP TO BE Worshipping ▶WARRIORS◀ WHO LIVE ADVENTUROUSLY, SATURATED IN HIS PRESENCE, & filled WITH HIS heart BEAT.

#MORE

chapter five
tasting GLORY

Growing up I always wanted *more.*

Boredom was not my friend.

I liked the faster lane of life—happy jaunts, bustling days, pining for fun.

Were you similar?

Remember the days of wondering, *Why do I have to make my bed?* The days when childhood chores confined us to a prisoner's existence? When chores were the dumbest idea in the world? So was brushing our teeth, taking a bath, and obeying rules—who has time for such things? We wanted to play! The goal, the aim, the fixation was for the next best taste of glory.

Did you know to engage God is to taste His glory? He's *fascinating.*

Remember the angels surrounding His throne in Isaiah's vision (Isa. 6:2)? From eternity past to eternity present they cannot get enough of Him. The beauty and brilliance of His majesty provokes a wonder they cannot shake. Nor do they want to. Their God does it for them. Surely they flap their wings in the highest praise for the loveliness and majesty set before them.

God, three-in-One, He is the *prize.*

I'm unsure if angels were created in their angelic makeup with a constant need to be pleasurably mystified; but we sure are. The discontent we often sense festering in us is not bad per se. It's what we do with our urges and surges to taste this glory we're looking for. Will we reach for goodness or filthiness in our pursuit to find pleasure?

If we lift up our heads and affix our eyes on the One who longs to satisfy us, the pursuit is saturated in the goodness of God. But if we place our aim on temporary satisfactions— even the best the world has to offer—we may find pleasure alright. But not the kind that promises pure joy. Nothing can supply us eternal pleasure without end but the Maker of heaven and earth.

In the last chapter, we discussed the value of healing and transformation. Why it's highly important for us to allow God the room to have His way in us entirely. But the question I want to answer in this chapter is: What comes after a season of healing and transformation?

I'd like to submit to you what comes after a season of healing and transformation is a greater enthrallment for the God who has shown Himself so wonderfully good to us.

At least that's my experience, anyway.

In the days when God was intently healing my heart, I often felt like He was doing cartwheels around me by showing off. Journeying back through the memories of my wounds was painful. Terribly painful! But the God holding my hand and leading me through it all kept soaking my heart in His love. God was so near, so attentive, and so comforting. The presence of God was unmistakable in those days. Everywhere I turned, I saw Him loving me, encouraging me, speaking words of life over me as if to say, "Keep going, dear one. I'm trustworthy."

As this season drew to a close, *I wanted Him more.*

$\mathcal{C}\!\sim$

What I learned from my own season of allowing God to heal my heart is, what God is doing is cleaning out the garden soil of our heart, and making us alive, tender, and sensitive to His presence. In this beautiful place of restoration God takes us from simply knowing Him to ushering us into having our eyes thrown open and our hair blown back by how fascinating He is.

Here's what I've learned about healing.

Healing prepares us for greater growth.

Healing give us our legs so we can run with, and after, God.

Healing lifts us up from the paralysis of our pain.

Healing sets us on a path to enjoy God.

There's a man in the book of Acts who is the epitome of what I'm talking about. This man hung around the temple gates in Jerusalem begging for handouts and help for years. Each day he rode people's backs as they dropped him off at the gate called Beautiful—he was lame from birth, and forty years old when God healed him.

Would you agree that's a mighty long time to be paralyzed?

What about being *close* to God's presence but untouched by Him?

Until, that is, the day hastened when God decided to blow the beggar's mind by miraculously supplying *more* than he ever thought to ask for.

Figuratively speaking, the beggar wanted a cup of water but God decided to give him the oceans. The beggar wanted mere sustenance for the day but God decided to give him a satisfaction beyond all understanding. God met the lame man in the middle of his paralyzing mess and offered him a miracle. God had a mind to give this hopeless man more than a simple offering so he could make it for another day. God desired to do such a wonder in this man's life that he'd rise to his feet fully alive and celebratory of his Lord.

Let's look at his story now:

Now Peter and John were going up together to the temple complex at the hour of prayer at three in the afternoon. And a man who was lame from birth was carried there and placed every day at the temple gate called Beautiful, so he could beg from those entering the temple complex. When he saw Peter and John about to enter the temple complex, he asked for help. Peter, along with John, looked at him intently and said, "Look at us." So he turned to them, expecting to get something from them. But Peter said, "I don't have silver or gold, but what I have, I give you: In the name of Jesus Christ the Nazarene, get up and walk!" Then, taking him by the right hand he raised him up, and at once his feet and ankles became strong. So he jumped up, stood, and started to walk, and he entered the temple complex with them—walking, leaping, and praising God. All the people saw him walking and praising God, and they recognized that he was the one who used to sit and beg at the Beautiful Gate of the temple complex. So they were filled with awe and astonishment at what had happened to him. (Acts 3:1–10)

I imagine his feet and ankles weren't all that was strengthened.

What about his faith in God's love for him?

Or his trust in God's goodwill toward broken people?

This reminds me of a time when I was young in my faith.

I desperately longed for another baby but due to severe, ongoing back pain, I was unable to carry a child. Through the prayers of His faithful servants, after years of suffering, God saw fit to heal my back.

After two years of horrendous pain, and a back surgery that left me more broken than before, the battle was over. No more pain pills, no more muscle relaxers, and no more having to lie down just to find relief.

Not only was this a big deal for my back, I had wanted another baby terribly bad. The doctors told me if I got pregnant there was nothing they could do for me. Furthermore, if I did get pregnant, I'd have to have a C-section since your tailbone moves during childbirth. But I was reading the Bible, and I was seeing God's supernatural, miraculous activity in people's lives. The more I read, the more God was using His Word to breathe faith into my spiritually young lungs. Sarah and Abraham were one of those stories—God giving them a baby when she was physically unable—and what I saw is that God is a God of the impossible.

Perhaps reading their story might encourage you too?

"Where is your wife Sarah?" they asked him. "There, in the tent," he answered. The LORD said, "I will certainly come back to you in about a year's time, and your wife Sarah will have a son!" Now Sarah was listening at the entrance of the tent behind him. Abraham and Sarah were old and getting on in years. Sarah had passed the age of childbearing. So she laughed to herself: "After I have become shriveled up and my lord is old, will I have delight?" But the LORD asked Abraham, "Why did Sarah laugh, saying, 'Can I really have a baby when I'm old?' Is anything impossible for the LORD? At the appointed time I will come back to you, and in about a year she will have a son." (Gen. 18:9–14)

The LORD came to Sarah as He had said, and the LORD did for Sarah what He had promised. Sarah became pregnant and bore a son to Abraham in his old age, at the appointed time God had told him. Abraham named his son who was born to him—the one Sarah bore to him—Isaac. When his son Isaac was eight days old, Abraham circumcised him, as God had commanded him. Abraham was 100 years old when his son Isaac was born to him. Sarah said, "God has made me laugh, and everyone who hears will laugh with me." She also said, "Who would have told Abraham that Sarah would nurse children? Yet I have borne a son for him in his old age." (Gen. 21:1–7)

Like Sarah's story, not only did God heal my back, He blessed my womb with Savannah too. I was so sure of God's healing touch that I went to the doctor for a pregnancy test within a month. When they took a urine culture, it came back negative. That's when I had them draw blood. *Bingo!* I was pregnant all right—God did the impossible!

Shock and awe.

God has more for you than the lame state life has left you in, my friend.

He loves you as is—no doubt. But, even so, He loves you far too much to allow you to stay there. Symbolically speaking, God has more for you than being carried around by others, begging for handouts. You were made for more—to know your God deeply and profoundly. Not just to know about Him—no, no. To enjoy His presence!

A. W. Tozer says it this way:

> The Presence and the manifestation of the Presence are not the same. There can be the one without the other. God is here when we are wholly unaware of it. He is manifest only when and as we are aware of His presence. On our part, there must be surrender to the Spirit of God, for His work is to show us the Father and the Son. If we cooperate with Him in loving obedience, God will manifest Himself to us, and that manifestation will be the difference between a nominal Christian life and a life radiant with the light of His face.[4]

Indeed, your God has a life of profound purpose prepared for you at the moment you take hold of His hand. If we'll come into agreement and say, "I follow close to You; Your right hand holds on to me" (Ps. 63:8). Then, just as God led His people out of the land of slavery in Egypt, He shall lead you.

> "For you are a people holy to the LORD your God. The LORD your God has chosen you to be a people for his treasured possession, out of all the peoples who are on the face of the earth. It was not because you were more in number than any other people that the LORD set his love on you and chose you, for you were the fewest of all peoples, but it is because the LORD loves you and is keeping the oath that he swore to your fathers, that the LORD has brought you out with a mighty hand and redeemed you from the house of slavery, from the hand of Pharaoh king of Egypt." (Deut. 7:6–8 ESV)

Would you like to know where taking His hand leads?

The answer is smack in the middle of the lame man's story.

Glance back at his account. What took place once he took Peter's hand?

It doesn't look huge but it is.

Did you notice the lame man not only stood to his feet, he walked into a lifestyle of walking with God? A lifestyle of worshipping God with everything he had? *He sure did.* Straight into the temple, into the sacred place of the presence of God.

That's what happens to a life God has profoundly set free from living in paralyzing bondage. We cannot help but to want to be near Him. We want to worship Him by learning about Him, enjoying His people, staying in His presence, and yielding to His beautiful continual work within us.

I believe after a mighty restorative work of God in our lives what comes next is an unparalleled season of growth. In this season of growth, God is raising us up to become worshipping warriors who live adventurously, saturated in His presence, and filled with His heartbeat. Not only for our own life, but also for those living all around us.

To do this, God, through the leadership of His Holy Spirit within us, takes us by the hand and begins to lead us into a life of wholehearted, reverential consecration. Because, as we saw in chapter 3, without holiness "no one will see the Lord."

To bask in the presence of God, we must surrender to a life of holiness since the Lord and His kingdom are pure, lovely, without sin and, gladly, untainted by this world.

To live a lifestyle of worship calls for the worshipper to endlessly give themselves over to the One they're worshipping. That's exactly what happened in my own life. It seemed like God required things of me that I didn't necessarily see Him require of my other Christian friends. For instance, God insisted I back off from running the mall so much and blowing off too much time shopping. He wanted me to take more time in not just reading my Bible—He wanted me to step it up, to begin digging deeper through learning how to study it. So, I signed up for a Bible study methods class at a local Christian college. I was scared out of my mind. I had not sat in a classroom since ninth grade. This fish was out of water. Can I even take a test or quiz? But God was pressing so I listened and obeyed.

God also required me to highly consider what I ingested through reading, listening to music, television and movies, and who I chose to spend time with. I ravenously read. Still do today. If words are around me I almost always read them. Cereal boxes, labels, what the person next to me on an airplane is reading. I'm obsessed. But God required I guard my eyes. What friends watched or read was not always mine to watch or read too.

Music was the same way. And that was challenging for this music lover. I almost always have music on. Even now, while writing to you, there is music playing. I love music. But

in my season of growth and consecration, God was purify-
ing my life—calling me to set myself totally apart for Him.

And lest you think for a second I had an attitude over
it, I did not. Not even close. I felt like a kid in a candy store.
Everywhere I turned God was there, in all sorts of delec-
table varieties. Sure, I could reach for chocolate-covered dog
food, but why would I want to when God was incomparably
better?

Looking back, I can clearly see the particular steps God
walked me through to mature in me the heart of a worshipping warrior.

It's funny because I'm often asked how I went from what
I was to what I am today. People want to know how I've
come to this place in life and ministry usefulness. Internally
I cringe because the awareness of my own humanity is ever
before me. A part of me wants to say what I know is true,
but it's not something most people desire to hear. In essence,
I lived under a Jesus rock. God required it of me, and sometimes I felt ridiculously embarrassed by it. Like those times
when people are quoting lines from well-known movies,
laughing, and carrying on, and I'm the idiot burning up in
embarrassment because the only lines I can quote are from
the pages of my Bible.

One time I remember feeling particularly embarrassed
by it and, talking to Erin, before I knew it I was bawling.
"But honey, I feel like I've lived under a Jesus rock all these
years and I don't know anything having to do with anything
but Jesus." To which he matter-of-factly replied, "And I wish
I was like you." I was taken aback.

Listen, if the Devil can't get us one way, he'll get us
another.

Feeling guilty for obeying God is pure stupidity.

So what if I lived under a Jesus rock?

Who really cares? Why should I?

False guilt can wear a soul out.

Let's keep throwing it off together, alright?

For the rest of this chapter let's look at some pertinent steps to walking with God daily. My hope is not only to shed light on how each one leads us further into attaining more of God, I hope you can see where God has you right now. Plenty of other faithful followers of Christ could supply you with their own version of the steps God has led them to walk with Him. All to say, these steps are not written in stone. I'm only sharing these for the benefit of helping you to find God in the way I can. Any wise Christian will tell you to study under many teachers, and to familiarize yourself with the presence of God and His revealed Word, the Bible.

Some steps overlap—that's normal. But to walk whole-heartedly in these principles will be what takes you from messy to miraculous in your pursuit of Christ and His presence.

Conviction

Conviction is the thing that brought me to God in the first place by the feelings of "needing to get right with God." Conviction of the Holy Spirit is what kept falling on me in the club.

It went like this—

First, a feverish pitch of angst would pummel me. Not the typical kind of anxiety I often struggled with, mind you. This was panic-attack material; leaving me stricken by a nauseous trepidation at the thought of working the floor, talking to customers, or anything else. I felt too paralyzed by fear to even leave the dressing room.

Next, a furious disdain for the industry would engulf my emotions. The ghetto girl inside me blazed of anger, she wanted to kick tail and take names. For things I'd seen, things I knew of, and things I ignorantly took part in; things like filth, and degradation, and outright injustice. I resented that I couldn't pack my bags, head for the door, and never don that disgusting establishment again. Had I been able to I would have. But no, I felt trapped. I had to work.

Then, a resentfulness toward the men would enrage me, while a slew of disturbing images flashed in my head like a strobe light. I almost couldn't take it. The perversion. The expectations. The beastly behaviors. The scores of married men. I wanted to scream, "Go home to your wife, you good-for-nothing loser!" Only I'd have added a few expletives back then, of course.

Last, the thought of their wives being stabbed in the back stabbed my heart too. Suddenly, my own self-disgust came alive. So much so, I'd viciously attack myself for being the trashy home-wrecking woman who participated in keeping such an evil fed.

Nothing was powerful enough to relieve that heavy load of misery crashing down on me. Not a personal pep talk, not a shot of liquid courage, and not a drug either. The only relief was to pack my bags, to call Erin, and to head back home.

The hardest part was I had no way to logically resolve this mess in my head. It made no sense, and I had no way of mentally contextualizing it. *It was baffling.*

Now I absolutely get it. Not only was I feeling the conviction of God's Spirit at my workplace, I was feeling it with Barbara. Conviction feels like guilt but is more than guilt; it's the Spirit of God saying, "This is the way to go. Walk in it." He's urging us to go to Him. Right this second. Yes, you are guilty. But if you'll go to Him, talk to Him about what's going on, and own up to whatever you need to own up to, He will grace you, forgive you, cleanse you, and empower you with newfound strength, resolve, and the continued awareness of His leadership in your life.

Conviction is feeling the drawing of God's presence in your life to surrender to Him in a particular way. Conviction is also the sorrow we feel when we fail to surrender to God.

Conviction is a beautiful gift from God that draws on our emotions for the sole purpose of bringing us back to where we belong: In the presence of God. Drenched in a wonder for God. Allowing His Spirit to purify us. Once He saturates us, He sets us free to run forth by lighting up our world for His fame and people's highest longing.

In short, when you feel that faint drawing on your heart to get right with God, to admit your sin, to say you're sorry, to seek Him more, that's conviction.

Listen to Him. *Immediately.* You'll find His life there.

Repentance

Repentance is getting raw honest with God. Talking to Him about what we're feeling. Hiding nothing. Withholding nothing. Throwing our guts up before God and getting the whole rotten mess out before Him. Repentance is how God cleanses the deepest places of our soul. It's also how He ushers forth the power of His Holy Spirit to transform our lowly selves into the likeness of His Son, Jesus Christ. Bypassing a lifestyle of true repentance before God will quench the Holy Spirit's available power from manifesting itself in our daily lives. Repentance keeps our house of worship (our bodies) clean and usable for God and His kingdom. If we want to stay aware and sensitive to God each day, living a lifestyle of repentance before Him is vital. Repentance is taking full responsibility for every thought, action, word, misdeed, and all areas of pride, self-reliance, ways we've not heeded God's conviction, or lack obeying Christ.

In short, repentance is buckling our knees to the authority and character of God. The moment we feel guilty. The second we sense the Spirit's "no-no" in our hearts. Instead of waiting until we "feel like it," we don't allow ourselves the room. Living a lifestyle of repentance is walking in step with the holiness of God today—right now.

Remember the time I lied to Erin and his family about my father? That's a prime example of not bending the knee in repentance when first convicted by the Spirit. God was convicting me to tell the truth, and I wasn't having it. I was too embarrassed to yield to God's conviction, to confess my sin in true authentic repentance. If I did then that meant I'd have to surrender to not only finding my dad, but I'd have to own up to lying. Are You kidding me, God? Please save me of the embarrassment.

The thing is, God allowed me to choose my own way but not barring consequences. If that was the direction I wanted to take, I could. But this was the consequence: the fullness of God's manifest presence wasn't participating. Not that He took His presence from me. He simply said, "Alright, I see what you want. You go ahead. I'm going to sit right here." And He did. He sat down, and sat quietly. Until I decided I'd had enough running around, doing my own thing.

Only thing is, doing my own thing was awfully lonely and unfulfilling. Repentance releases the pent-up dam for a fresh release of the presence of God. It restores the joy of our salvation, and the oneness we delight in with His Spirit, and hunger to have more of, with God.

Repentance also secures us from living in the wide-open territory of the enemy's camp. Walking in a lack of holiness to God and habitual sin removes from us, to some measure, the protection of God because what we've done is taken sides with the Enemy against our God. We have willingly come into agreement with Satan's purposes, plans, and will for our lives, therefore, we are free game for him to lead us astray, to torment us, and to seduce our head full of lies leading us to destruction. Satan's biggest game is to seduce us into self-destructing ourselves. Repentance secures our safety, restores our vision, and opens the lines of communication and intimacy between God and us. Living a lifestyle of repentance is vital. Repentance brings down the walls separating us from God.

Teachability

Having a teachable heart is vital for knowing God more, for keeping what we've already attained in Him, and for actively engaging with God from day to day—even being used by Him. Having a teachable disposition before God not only blesses Him, it allows Him to use us in greater measures. Why is this so? Because the one who has a teachable heart is yielding to His conviction by surrendering themselves fully; plus, they are showing signs of great humility and obviously yielding in repentance before Him too. Those who are teachable get to enjoy the secret things of God because they've proven themselves trustworthy enough to share His heart with. When we walk with God, His ways are not like our ways. We must yield to His leadership, His way of doing things, Him calling the shots and us simply following. But oh when we follow. This is where the "more" is found.

In my own life, like I told you already, God required more of me than He seemed to require of others. Now, whether that was true or not is subjective to my own narrow-minded insight. In all honesty, we never fully know what God is doing in another person. Truth is, they could be under the same levels of conviction as us but in other areas. One cannot see. What do we know?

Having a teachable heart is looking to God as our source of life, not comparing ourselves with others to the right or to the left. Seeing what they're learning, doing, or not doing. Our eyes are on the Great Teacher, not pinging here and there and everywhere, giving us a serious case of spiritual A.D.D. Having a teachable heart is a willingness to listen to our Instructor and to do what He says—and the sooner the better for God to receive highest worship and our greatest joy.

Intercession

Intercession is living in a place of open dialogue with God for you and for others. Where conviction draws us to God, intercession keeps us before God. It positions Him in the most prominent place for everything pertaining to life, to godliness, to His will and work in our lives, as well as His will and work in others. If a crisis comes up and we turn to God in prayers, calling on Him to act, throwing the situation and circumstances before Him, that's intercession. Intercession is more than the simple act of praying but it's throwing all things before Him and calling on Him to move, to act, to intervene, and to respond. Intercession is not about having polished and primped prayers for others to be impressed by. Intercession is living a humble life before God, welcoming Him into every area of our lives and the lives we are bringing before Him, and keeping our ear to His chest to hear His heartbeat. Intercession is not just praying; it's listening for His plans, purposes, and areas where He is inviting us to join Him in the work He has in mind and desires to do.

Like the time I was specifically praying for Erin in the quietness of my closet. I was earnestly praying for his salvation—even frustrated. God was making Himself quite obvious. So I begged God, "What in the world is the problem? I don't understand." Little did I know, God was about to speak. As I came out of the closet, I was about to make my bed when all of a sudden a Scripture verse flashed in my mind's eye—Ezekiel 12:1. Being new to the Bible, I was clueless what it said. That's when I said out loud to the Lord, "Lord, if this is You talking to me, I'm about to freak out." Right about then I saw my Bible lying on the bedside table. As my heart was beating out of my chest, I went and opened it to Ezekiel 12:1–2: "The word of the LORD came to me: 'Son of man, you are living among a rebellious house. They have eyes to see but do not see, and ears to hear but do not hear, for they are a rebellious house.'" I screamed, and nearly ran a lap in my room! What in the world? God blew my mind. He also gave me exactly what to begin praying over my husband. This is one way how intercession works.

What God was teaching me was how to get on the same page with Him so I could align more fully to praying specifically—according to how God sees things. Some say intercession is a gift some are given by the Holy Spirit, and others are not. Although, I agree to a certain point, I beg to differ too. Granted, some people are houses of prayer walking around on two legs. Like my friend, Shannon, or another woman I love, Mary Ann. Don't dare ask these women to pray unless you mean it because they will and they take it seriously. Both of these women live to pray and pray to live. They live keenly aware of the presence of God and always seem on point to how God seems to be moving around them.

Do they have a special gifting or anointing on their life for prayer? *Yes.*

However, I do think you and I can grow to become more like them, and God wants us to.

In short, intercession is leaving the shallow shores of "God bless our food, our lives, and our dog," for the much rougher waters where God is teaching us "to will and to work for his great pleasure" (Phil. 2:13 ESV). Even the deeper waters of praying for ourselves: "God, if You do not keep my head above water, I won't make it." Or the deep waters of praying for our families: "God, if You do not keep all of us treading these dangerous waters, we're all sure to die. You alone are our only Help, our greatest victory, and our ultimate joy. In Jesus' mighty, saving, powerful name."

ᶜ∽

So there we have it. Each step could be its own book, actually. I could've written for days. But that's not the goal, nor my intention. My prayer is to help set you to your feet and start to journey down the road with God a little further. To offer help from my own daily walk of learning how to stay connected with God, sensing His presence all around, and doing His work.

Conviction pricks us by setting us to our feet.

Repentance cleanses us by strengthening our ankles and legs.

Teachability keeps us in step with the Holy Spirit.

Intercession clears our vision to see as the Spirit sees.

This is the lifestyle of a worshipping warrior—tasting glory.

One who cannot get enough of God because He's so fascinating.

god SEES THE WHOLE picture & MAKES HIS CONCESSIONS BASED ON WHAT HIS POWER CAN DO. #MORE

chapter six

SUPERFICIAL faith

All manner of sufferings broke loose after I wrote a proposal for this book. I marinated on this concept for months before I scribbled any outlines or attempted my hand at summary sentences. Then, as I've told you already, my pretty church-girl world blew up.

Now I can see God was on a warpath taking a whip to the religious hypocrisy I had slowly and unknowingly given myself over to. I was clueless that I was being deceived. Nor did I realize I had bowed down to an idol of "easy, simple, peace at all cost, religious rule following and keeping people happy." The slyness of following religious expectations landed me flat on my face, sucking wind, and barely making it.

I became a hardened, angry, resentful, depressed, victim full of chaos again.

What in the world happened to this mess-made-miracle?

I drank the poison of hypocrisy—of dual Christianity—by believing one thing and living another. Somewhere, somehow I bowed down to believing I needed to be a good church girl instead of a woman in love with her God—it was grievous idolatry. Doing "this" and not "that" drove me to religious irrationality, and it drained my faith utterly dry. However, had you called me a hypocrite I had plenty of good excuses for my actions.

In fact, you might have apologized for saying such a thing because clearly, I know God.

Do you even know what a mess God has saved me from?

I am, after all, a miracle. How *dare* you make such a harmful accusation?

Furthermore, can you not see how much God is doing in my life?

Aren't people's lives being changed?

I study the Bible every day. I pray all the time. I listen to worship music constantly.

Do you not see how closely I walk with God? How teachable I am?

I teach a thriving weekly class; exegetical teaching—steak, not milk.

I listen to preaching podcasts all the time.

I bury my head in biblical resources to educate myself—a ravenous pupil of God.

Nothing like your world falling apart to see your pride!

I believe God desired I write this message from a fresh state of brokenness.

I've come to see once again how freshly broken vessels offer advice much differently than those who haven't had to drink a cup of desperation in a while. We're liable to get blinded by our self-righteousness and think of fellow strugglers, "Good grief. Get it together. How hard is it anyway?"

Then God allows a good hard sifting to beat the pride right out of us.

Years ago I was diagnosed with hypothyroidism. If you're unfamiliar with the workings of the thyroid, it monitors all things metabolism in our systems. Because my thyroid is underactive without medicinal help, if I forget to take my medicine for a few days, sleepiness and a depressive mood starts setting in. Before long, I'm sluggish, lethargic, and unable to think clearly. Sometimes I even find myself driving through Starbucks more frequently to give me some pep in the afternoons, and to keep me from dozing at the wheel while running errands or heading home from work.

However, if my thyroid is regularly getting the proper doses of medicine, I can run circles around my twenty-two-year-old daughter. Sometimes she says to me after a long day together, "Oh my goodness, I need a nap! How are you not tired?"

"Um, let's see, because I am *the* woman that's how." . . . To which we crack up.

In all seriousness, this is exactly what happens in the spiritual realm without regular doses of the Lord's presence in our lives, as well as constant reminders of what Jesus' sacrifice and resurrection have afforded us as His beloved children. God's presence and regular doses of the gospel message metabolize our physical and spiritual systems.

I know we've talked about what the Good News of the gospel is already. But let's take a look at it one more time while asking this question: What is the Good News?

Here, let me condense it down into something we can all understand.

- The Good News is Jesus Christ loves and saves sinners, even the worst of all.
- The Good News is we don't have to clean ourselves up for God; that's His part.
- The Good News is we don't have to stay bound to our sinful nature anymore—we are free—when we put our entire faith in Jesus' shed blood on the cross to save us.

⌒

In all honesty, if we are not consistently ingesting the medicine of the Good News, we will become spiritually sluggish, lethargic, and unable to think clearly. Our hearts will eventually feel lackluster—even depressed—because the bent of our inclinations has turned inward instead of upward. Truth is, when you and I take the place of God in our lives—through not seeking God's presence—we morph into whiney, wimpy brats who get consumed with ourselves.

Interestingly, this is exactly what happens when we fall physically sick. Have you noticed how hard it is to not think of yourself and wish everyone would baby you when you aren't feeling good? Our sights take on a jadedness when our realm of view becomes me, myself, and I. However, when our sights are set upon the Lord Jesus Christ, relief comes—on Jesus, crucified, and risen on our behalf.

But it doesn't end there.

Jesus also shared His resurrection power with His children, and those who choose to believe what His death and resurrection have secured for them find incredible fulfillment in their journey with Him. And, I'd venture to say, it's these children who run circles around other Christians, living a life in Christ few truly find. They are the ones who find Peter's words true in their own experience with Christ when he says in 2 Peter 1:3–4, "His divine power has given us everything required for life and godliness through the knowledge of Him who called us by His own glory and goodness. By these He has given us very great and precious promises, so that through them you may share in the divine nature, escaping the corruption that is in the world because of evil desires."

So what sets these apart from the rest? I'd say a continued willingness to keep falling facedown before the Lord God in a state of unusual surrender. These people are willing to admit they are not God, nor do they want to be. They don't have a problem taking a beggar's stance before a holy God. And it's these, by a miraculous work of the Spirit's power, who live transformed into remarkable, courageous saints. What sets these apart is they've learned to bow themselves quickly and consistently to the God of the gospel message.

What I want us to understand is merely going to church on Sundays and genuinely walking with God daily are two different entities that are in opposition to one another.

The one who walks with God daily says, "Jesus Christ is Lord and Savior of my life, my eternal joy, and what anchors everything about me."

The other goes to church on Sunday's for self-esteem, so as to feel better about one's self.

One gives up her rights, swallowed up in a life of devotion to Jesus.

The other exercises the right of pretense, looking good to themselves, and possibly a few others.

One says by their actions, "All my life is Yours, Lord Jesus."

The other is saying, "Look at me, aren't I good?"

Before I step on your toes too much, I better confess right now, I've been both.

I remember when I first began seeking God, and all of my close friends were still as lost as a goose. The day I got baptized, I took to those baptismal waters with an invisible badge of honor fixed to my chest. Looking back, I was so puffed up, strutting my stuff like a peacock. I loved people seeing this good deed I did, being a church girl and all.

This all proved empty a few weeks later when I wasn't any different than before. Even the four weeks of foundation classes, afterwards, didn't change me. All that strut did nothing but make me feel like a big ole hypocrite among my friends. Though the inward seeking of God was genuine, the need to be seen by others was nothing but a form of bondage.

May I ask you a few probing questions?

How much of your seeking of God and serving in church life is genuine?

How much is, like me, nothing but strut?

The place where our messy lives transform into miraculous lives is when we truly surrender our lives to being authentic daughters of God—when we lose our strut and trade it in for full immersion into a relationship with Jesus Christ.

Some of us need to bow out of roles, relationships, leadership responsibilities, and areas of service in order to arise from our captivity to others' opinions of us, and the continuous stroking of our pride. In doing so, we'll begin living the release to freedom Jesus has promised to those who believe. As long as we stay with our feet rooted in needing the inward stroke of the soul to fulfill us and give us identity, we will live as captives. And, sadly, we will stay bound to our messiness regardless of how well we appear to others.

I experienced a tad of this firsthand not too long ago. I was sensing God saying to my heart, "Lay down your class," and I was scared to death. I had taught this Sunday school class each week for a little over six years. I was greatly troubled. I was scared to let down those in leadership, who had taken the time to invest in me. Nor did I want to disappoint the women in my class whom I loved with an utmost affection.

I was raised to serve my local church before going outside of my church to do any public ministry. And I feared being disobedient to this advice. But God was leading otherwise. And He meant business.

Interestingly, I was teaching the Gospel of Luke, and we were moving to a place where we were seeing the disciples leaving all to follow Jesus. I was cut to the core when God suddenly took what I was teaching my class and turned it around on me.

Would I leave all to follow Him?

Would I practice what I was teaching?

Is my faith superficial or super-faithful?

Sadly, it took my husband having a crisis to get me to finally obey. The day I walked in and told the leadership I was stepping down was cathartic. I cried my eyes out, and felt terrible for putting them in a place of spinning their wheels, trying to figure things out. But I couldn't disobey God any longer. Looking back, I wish I had listened earlier. I hate that I took months to obey the voice of the Lord—He is worthy of so much more. I also hate the notion it took all hell breaking loose in my private world to get me there, but it did. Nevertheless, I wasn't prepared for what would happen soon afterward.

Suddenly, when I didn't have a class anymore, I started questioning my identity and purpose. I hadn't realized how much of my identity and purpose in life had become tied to what I did each week. It would take months to untangle the mess I slipped into, but God was restoring me to who I really was, and that's His. Above and beyond what any of us do in areas of service or life descriptions, what is foundational and unshakable is we are God's children. This alone is where we find our purpose and identity. Not in what we do, but in Whose we are.

Some of us stay in our messes because the mess does something for us. It fluffs our need for approval of man—where we are getting something out of it. And we can't imagine this being removed because of the unknown mysterious void it would create in our lives.

But please allow me to speak some truth over you. This satisfaction is temporary, and you are, like Isaiah 44:20 says, one who "feeds on ashes." You are deceived and holding on to a lie. You are dying slowly. There isn't light at the end of this tunnel. No, what's ahead is more captivity, more purposelessness, and more confusing darkness. Cords are tying around your neck, and the Enemy is looking for just the right time to yank them tight so he can choke out whatever life is in you. Thankfully, when Jesus lives in you, the Devil cannot fully snuff out all life because your Savior will never leave you nor forsake you. But, your disobedience has invited a ravaging unlike anything you've known thus far. Satan, as the Bible teaches, has taken you captive to do his will (2 Tim. 2:26).

Here are some other ways Satan takes us captive to do his will.

Staying safe, which leads to boredom. Life with Christ is nothing short of an adventure. It's risk, risk, and risk some more. If we're bored, somewhere along the way we took the bait of safety and quit risking. Are we bold in our faith? Doing the hard thing? Walking courageously for Christ? Surrendering our entire lives? Truly needing and subsisting on Jesus? If not, it's time to repent and return wholeheartedly, my friend.

Staying busy, which leads to ineffectiveness. Who isn't chasing their tail these days? If we're not pushing back on busyness, it's got us. Oddly enough though, too much productivity makes us ineffective. How so? Sitting and soaking in God's presence renews us and makes us most effective. Without these concentrated times, we're empty and have nothing of value to give. That's why the Enemy hounds us with distractions to keep us busy instead of seeking the Lord. He knows the danger. He knows what we fixate on is what we worship. Resist him; sit and soak with your Savior.

Staying self-focused, which leads to captivity. The day we came to Christ, the prison doors opened up. No longer a slave to the sinful nature. Given eyes to see past our prior blindness. Fashioned into a brand-new creation. The Enemy's game here is dulling our senses to anything that speaks of our freedoms. Perhaps this is why we feel like failures. It looms over us, like a dark, thick cloud. Stand to your feet and renounce the lies of the Enemy with the verses from Luke 4:16–21—the gospel of Good News.

Interestingly, there's a lot of talk among Christian circles these days about the gospel. But as I look around I'm also noticing very few of us actually live what the gospel preaches. In all of our pious and profound explanations of the gospel, are we helping people to freedom in Christ? At the end of the day, is our preaching and teaching helping to open the prison doors for those bound to their sinful natures and living in addictive sin?

Oh, what danger when we quit beholding Jesus!

Did you know the Lord has a masterpiece in mind when He looks at you?

Every fragmented piece of your life—is His artwork in the making.

Every area where you've suffered pain—He's looking to make whole.

In the Master's hands, heaps of ashes become displays of His beauty. The rigid become tender. The hardened become full of life. No life is deemed unworthy. God uses what the world labels as foolish to confound the wise. You're welcome at a feasting table of grace.

Jesus walked this earth lowering Himself into the likes of a servant, a humble man who enjoyed food and rich conversations in the homes of tax collectors and sinners. This infuriated the religious leaders. They were much too high on their spiritual horses to stoop so low as to fellowship with *those* people. But Jesus' love was made manifest when He took the time to heal the hurting, notice the rejects, the sinners, the lepers and, even, the harlots.

What sets Jesus apart is His ability to see through the eyes of redemption. He's not so much looking at the mess. He's looking at the masterpiece. He's not so much concerned with who we've been, but who we'd become if we wholeheartedly put our faith in Him.

But make no mistake.

Our past is never, ever, ever wasted. It is a tool of purpose in the hand of a very strategic God if we'll humble ourselves to become fully healed vessels. Because Jesus is the Alpha and Omega, the beginning and the end, He doesn't place the same limited assumptions on our identities like we do. You and I judge with limited information. But God sees the whole picture and makes His concessions based on what His power can do. It's a faith, if you will, in His ability to execute impossibilities.

Have you needed this truth like a cold drink of water on a hot summer day?

Some of us have lost our way in the cold, boring halls of religion. And it's time we came out of captivity, again. We might have landed here with good intentions. Perhaps pursuing religious studies—only to find ourselves chained up in not knowing what to believe anymore. Somehow along the way something changed when we exchanged our sincere devotion for Christ for a shriveled up version of faith.

Truth is, all the studying can drain us of the life-giving power of God, and wad us up in confusions and conflicts.

Have you become defensive, arrogant, and full of spiritual pride?

Maybe even argumentative, thinking you've needed to defend God?

It's possible you might be thinking you're defending the gospel. And you very well could be. But are your intentions pure? Hold out your motivations under the light of truth. It's always wise to see if we're defending the gospel, or merely defending our version of the gospel—a version stained with religious pride.

We must guard against a religious critical spirit.

Let's always run back to our first love.

Some of us have lost our way in perpetual self-infatuation. We talked about this in chapter 3. However, in this context I think it's worthy to bring up again. We've become more self-aware than God-aware. What we're suffering from is a classic case of narcissism, and we don't even know it. We suffer under loads of self-focus—obsessing over our insecurities, constantly focusing on our sinful natures and what scum of the earth we are, or comparing ourselves to others and coming up ahead or falling short—where our gaze is constantly us-ward and inward.

It's all a version of self-infatuation.

Again, true faith begins and ends with God as the grand subject. Our lives should be about feeding on God's Word, which says we are loved, cherished, worthy, adopted children of the Most High God, who are filled with His presence and more than conquerors in this dark and dingy world. If we were loved enough for Jesus to crawl on a cross and die for us, it's time we start walking in the resurrection life He's come to give us. The voices of condemnation are keeping us bound in nothing but a narcissistic mentality. And the Good News of the gospel is Jesus has set us free! We aren't victims any longer. No, we are victorious in Christ!

Transformation out of the mess comes when we fix our eyes on Christ. When we take Jesus' hand of help and give Him the freedom to pull us out of the pit of self-pity. When our inward gaze turns upward, this is where we find sweet relief from our constant preoccupation with ourselves.

Picking ourselves apart to pieces doesn't bring freedom from the slavery of sin. It enslaves us all the more. Why? We're suffocated by our powerlessness to change our lives.

&

Recently, I sat among a group of women. I came to this group barely limping along as I shared at the beginning of our journey together. One woman whom God is raising up in our generation was fearful she'd steal God's glory as she stepped out to serve Him. My eyes widened as a sister from another denomination remarked, "I seriously don't understand your thinking. Will you please help me understand?" She honestly didn't get the theology behind her sister's confession. When she asked a few more penetrating questions, I was struck. "Isn't God big enough to slam your face to the ground if you begin stealing His glory? Why do you focus on yourselves so much? God is my focus. What He's called me to do. The people He's called me to serve. That's what is on my mind."

It struck me because I understood both sides.

One felt stuck in the messy; the other felt free in the miraculous.

One focuses on her sin; the other on her victory in Christ.

One's afraid she'll make a mistake; the other is so full of faith she could bust.

Suddenly, I remembered being the "other" kind of believer.

I remembered being so overwhelmed by God, so overwhelmed with His deep love for people, so burdened for the lost living around me, and so consumed with Jesus' desire to heal the broken. So much so, I lived free from the enslaving chains of self-awareness.

And you know what?

Lives were touched by Jesus and set free.

When people were bound in darkness, I'd lay my hands on them and pray full of faith, believing God's will was to set captives free. And guess what? Jesus set them free! The lost were being found. The blind were seeing. And I wasn't living a brand of Christianity that's so safe it never sees God move anymore. I was seeing Jesus working miracles and wonders because my faith was aflame with the abiding power and presence of God. And it wasn't because I was seeking His hand and not His face. It was because I believed what I was reading; mixing my faith with what He was saying to do.

I wasn't just reading great stories from the Bible of saints who walked with God. To the contrary, I was living a great story by being the one who walked with God. Somewhere along the way I ended up in the wilderness desert of unbelief. However, I dropped to my knees before my colaborers in Christ proclaiming, "I'm going with God; no matter the cost."

Would you like to know why this was so huge?

Because going with God costs.

Going with God has never been popular. Sadly, even among families and church folks.

I wouldn't be the least bit surprised if you happen to know exactly what I am talking about. Like me, have you felt the sting of loneliness that being a follower of Christ can bring? Perhaps in a dear relationship? Maybe even at work among coworkers?

The bottom line is not everyone is as enthusiastic as we are about us changing the course of our spiritual direction by becoming more intentional in our relationship with Christ. For one, our loved ones can oftentimes feel a sense of betrayal whether they're able to articulate it as betrayal or not. Or, two, our newfound spirituality can trigger religious insecurities—insecurities they're not too sure what to make of.

What is more, sometimes veering off to follow Christ wholeheartedly means we bring a measure of controversy into our spheres of influence. Like our workplaces. For instance, the lack of integrity we've been walking in? God says, "No more." Or how about the lunchroom gossip, slander, and backbiting? This, too, must stop. And what about wasting our employers time and resources by indulgent socializing and having a poor work ethic? God says, "Enough of that business." To our Lord, even our work is worship. God certainly cares.

I've realized recently how walking with God is controversial. And the minute we make "not being controversial" our goal, we better sit down. Even Jesus came under massive amounts of scorn. Why wouldn't we? Being called a religious fanatic by our unbelieving family members is to be expected.

Since when did we let this bother us so?

And for those of us who are leaders brave enough to run with God in our generation, please allow me to encourage you. Much of the religious elite in Jesus' day had problems with His theology, and those in our day with pharisaical hearts will have problems with ours. Don't be surprised. Don't for a minute take a victim stance and allow resentment or bitterness to set in; but you also shouldn't let them bully you into staying safe and spiritually politically correct.

If fear is consuming you these days, fall on your face and confess it to God. Then, ask His Spirit to yank that mess off of you. He will!

It seems the same spirit that's in our political systems has gotten into the church. Today's Christian news feeds read very similar to today's political news feeds. There's so much arguing going on, it's nauseating. There's division, strife, fear, and far too much pride over who is and isn't "right."

Both sides have scowls on their faces brooding over each other's faults.

Dear one, let's return to the biblical truth that the world should know us by our love for Jesus and our love for one another. There is a way to disagree. Arguing, malicious talk, public shaming without prior conversations, and attempts of mutual understanding isn't biblical according to God's Word.

Let's decide today we aren't compromising.

Let's wage war with love.

There's great value in seducing Christians to live on their high horse. This kind of thinking exalts theology while reducing the love of God. Satan roars wildly about, hoping to wad us up with any distraction—even religious ones. It's time to quit taking the bait by returning to our first love. To the One who once took our breath away. The One who once made our hearts leap for joy over such a wondrous salvation. Satan stepped in and maligned our way. His goal was to usurp God's glory. But I say to you today, "Arise, shine, for your light has come" (Isa. 60:1).

Get back up and run to your Redeemer. His arms are wide open. Run to a place where you can be alone, and fall on your face before God. Cry out to Him in your disobedience, asking Him for forgiveness. After you've fully repented, pray for God's mercy to deliver you from this awful place—where you've given the Enemy limited authority over you through your disobedience.

Then, begin situating yourself anew in the presence of God like you never have before! You need the Holy Spirit to saturate your desert soul. You've been dry, and the Living Water desires to well up to overflowing in your life.

Don't believe the lie that after disobedience, coming back to Jesus will take a long time. When you run to your Lord with earnest desperation, He can receive you and restore you quicker than you suspect. He longs to have the fullness of wonderful fellowship with you. He means for you and Him to be close. He won't hold your disobedient ways against you when you ask for His forgiveness and fully return your whole life to Him. Our Lord is the celebratory Father of the prodigal. His coat anticipates clothing you, with a ring and a party to follow. This isn't a time to keep a cowardly, shameful stance. Now is not the time to come up with a thousand excuses for why He shouldn't love you or forgive you. This is a time to let God's wild grace wash over you. Now is a time to stand under the fount of redeeming love, which turns every mistake into a miracle of redemption.

All of us are desperate for this kind of encounter with the presence of God. So much comes to distract us from sitting before Him often and experiencing it, though. Oftentimes, we will move into this realm but only for a few days.

Why is this so?

For one, it takes added work.

We don't know how to un-busy ourselves well—it's abnormal. But when we do, the joy we're unaccustomed to takes form in our hearts and we start to really believe that, "God is most glorified in us when we are most satisfied in Him."[5] What's happening is we're tapping into real, live satisfaction.

But, have you ever noticed how as quickly as it begins, it ends?

Somehow you start physically not feeling well, or you get busy with something suddenly pressing your schedule. Perhaps your boss requires a little more time at the office. Or your kids start acting out of control. Maybe unexpected guests come to town and need a place to stay. Whatever the reason, you cannot seem to continue seeking the Lord like you were.

Don't be fooled, my friend. Remember the spiritual warfare stuff we talked about in chapter 3? Yep, more than likely, this is exactly what's at play. Satan will use almost anything to divert our attention elsewhere. And if we don't know how to stand against distractions, we won't.

You've tapped into the very reason God created you—for intimacy with your Creator. And the Devil's mad. He doesn't want you beholding your Lord too much. For he knows God will gain too much glory from your life. Why? Because those who behold their Maker become fascinated with Him! And the desire is placed within our souls to be more like Him. This stirs up great anger for Satan. What a slap in the face to the very one who wanted to be God.

As co-heirs of Christ, we share in our Father's glorious identity.

Did you know He calls us lovely, holy, and worthy?

The Enemy's greatest disgust is when flawed sinners become faultless saints.

So what do you say we give him some grief? How about we do as Hebrews 12:1–2 says:

> Therefore, since we also have such a large cloud of witnesses surrounding us, let us lay aside every weight and the sin that so easily ensnares us. Let us run with endurance the race that lies before us, keeping our eyes on Jesus, the source and perfecter of our faith, who for the joy that lay before Him endured a cross and despised the shame and has sat down at the right hand of God's throne.

How about we look fully into our Lord's beautiful face?
How about we throw off the restraints?
How about we lay aside our reputations?
How about we lose ourselves in the pursuit of Christ?

IF
authentic
JOY
AND
Adventure
IS WHAT YOU WANT IN LIFE,
THE WAY YOU GET THERE
IS FOLLOWING God's
LEAD.
#MORE

chapter seven

Worshipping WARRIORS

I'd venture to say we've entered a time on the kingdom calendar when people are sick of the status quo. Church isn't what we wish it was. Something isn't quite right. And we're ready for change. Those of us in leadership are tired of the religious bullies standing guard against anything that has a hint of, can I say, New Testament authenticity? We keep reading the Bible, but our eyes glaze over because it isn't at all what we're experiencing. We may even be asking ourselves, "Is my faith even real?"

Such was the season in my own life when I began the process of writing this book. I was hitting the top of my game by my denomination's ministry standards. The Sunday morning class I was teaching was growing. Beth Moore, America's beloved Bible teacher, had taken me under her wing and was mothering and mentoring me in the faith. LifeWay Christian Resources published a Bible study I wrote. Churches were calling me to come and speak to their women. *But something was slowly unraveling in me.*

With all this newfound favor, my own relationship with Jesus was growing increasingly stale. I realize now I was too busy doing kingdom work instead of seeking the Great God and King Himself. I wasn't able to admit this at the time. I was honestly deceived by the notion that I was "doing what God had called me to do." Truth is, by all outward examinations, I was totally and completely enthralled with the Lord. But I know now I was more consumed with studying Scripture to prepare for lessons, and write materials, and making sure I had something to say to women—more than simply loving Jesus for myself. I'd become so busy in ministry, my praying was from a stance of, "God, help me!" instead of "Lord, I love you."

I needed a serious wake-up call. And I got it.

I was knee-deep in the Gospel of Luke when I started seeing what a mess I'd become. And it *undid* me. For two solid years my Sunday morning Bible study and I journeyed in a thorough exegesis of Luke's account of the life and ministry of Jesus. I don't think any of us were prepared for how much the lessons would step on our toes. The life Scripture calls us to seize and the ones we actually were living didn't match. We were sobered to the core. Beginning with the teacher. It wasn't real pretty.

What I saw in my daily studies of the Gospel of Luke is most of us live a far different experience in Christ than those we read about in the Bible, especially from the pages of the New Testament. And one thought wouldn't get off my mind: *If God were writing a modern-day list of people who walked in biblical faith likened to the lives of those in Hebrews 11, would I make the cut?* Would *any* of us make the cut? I was ruined because I knew the answer. I then fell on my face before the Lord, pleading for my own forgiveness.

We are settling for so much less than Jesus died on the cross to give us.

Sure we believe we're forgiven. Sure we believe we're loved. Sure we believe we've received mercy. But do we believe we're empowered with the Spirit of God to light our world on fire? Do we believe we can live a life ablaze with the presence and power of God from day-to-day? Are we changing our world for His glory?

I think not, and we desperately need transformation.

It began dawning on me how nowhere in the New Testament Scriptures do I see a single place where you and I are given permission to believe we're given to a life of barely making it, for one day we'll all be in heaven and we won't have to deal with our flesh natures anymore. This is not the life Christ has called us to live. Never do I see permission for us to live as wretches, constantly controlled and beaten down by our flesh natures.

What I see is a bunch of apostles calling us to thrive on the gospel message of full redemption and to advance God's kingdom on this earth. I see a band of apostles who issued a serious call for all believers to utterly abandon their lives for their God. What I see is a bunch of men who knew Christ and knew who they were *in Christ*.

For we must not forget a former murderer, the apostle Paul, penned these words to the Romans, "Therefore, no condemnation now exists for those in Christ Jesus, because the Spirit's law of life in Christ Jesus has set you free from the law of sin and of death" (Rom. 8:1–2). Not only did the apostle Paul understand we must not put up with condemnation, he also saw, amid our struggles and sufferings, it is not God's intention for us to live as clots of flesh barely making it by on this earth when he also said, "No, in all these things we are more than victorious through Him who loved us" (Rom. 8:37).

In fact, the apostle Paul tells us in Colossians 3:1–3 to get busy by setting our minds on the things above: "If then you have been raised with Christ [to a new life, thus sharing His resurrection from the dead], aim at and seek the [rich, eternal treasures] that are above, where Christ is, seated at the right hand of God. And set your minds and keep them set on what is above (the higher things), not on the things that are on the earth. For [as far as this world is concerned] you have died, and your [new, real] life is hidden with Christ in God" (AMP).

I hate to say this, and it's not something we love to hear, but most of us have been seduced by the Enemy into walking in a serious case of *disbelieving what God says*. And we're miserable. It's taken our life and legs out from under us.

Before you balk at me and lay down this book, we see this in the same chapter of Hebrews on the topic of faith when Paul said, "Now without faith it is impossible to please God, for the one who draws near to Him must believe that He exists and rewards those who seek Him" (Heb. 11:6).

So how do we begin changing? I'm so glad you asked.

It begins with a full-on return to the presence of God.

That's why we've pounded the point of *surrender.*

If we want to run after the *more* of God, surrender is key.

Oh friend, God is up to something in our day. Are you sensing it? There's a rumbling! There's a shaking! From the east, to the west, the north and the south—God is calling His people to arise. To shake off the chains! To throw off yokes of religious strivings! To stand up with our Savior and give Him every vestige of rule over us by giving Him the authority to deal a deathblow to our wretchedness of sinfulness! Because He went through the trouble of emptying Himself. Taking on the form of a servant. A helpless baby. Needing burping, and diapering, and taught and taken care of by the very ones He had created. Can you even imagine? Not only that, He opened Himself to our insults, our rejections, the sick spit from our mouths and, then, the brutal crucifixion of His innocent body on a cross. All to save us! All because of His love for us! Church, God is calling us to set our eyes like flint back upon the Author and Finisher of our faith who is for us and not against us, who is King and Master and Sovereign Lord over all.

What if we *finally* took back what the Enemy has stolen—the surrendered ground?

What is the surrendered ground?

Would you not say it's the freedom provided through the death and resurrection of Jesus Christ? Freedom from the captivity of sinfulness and separation from intimacy with our Creator God? Would you not say it's our freedom in every area of our lives—emotionally, relationally, physically, mentally, and spiritually?

Satan is robbing us of the gorgeous restoration of a living, breathing, God-glorifying, celebratory lavishness in His presence of everything the Good News of the gospel provides. But if authentic joy and adventure is what you want in life, the way you will get there is to follow God's lead. Walking with Him isn't for wimps; it's for warriors who are willing to lay down their life to a single-minded, whole-hearted, devotion in worshipful reverence.

This is the lifestyle of a worshipping warrior.

If we want more of God we must let God do more in us.

Let's be honest.

All of us have a messy spot in our lives that's dying for a miraculous touch from God.

Whether this mess is an unfixable relationship or an unfixable emotion or, even, perhaps a reputation we've acquired. Though we've done a ton of changing, we're still experiencing the mounds of suffocating shame. Like one friend I know who isn't at all what people envision her to be. The one some folks have in their head is not who they think she is. No, she only acted out because of underlying pain. If people knew the root of her actions they might show her a little compassion. Then again, maybe not. Some people are happy to see us in a ditch rather than giving us a hand up. Sad, but true. If this has been your supposed fair share of a lot, I apologize for the pain it's caused you. I hate this for you. However, I know Someone who hates it more.

God.

I hope you're getting a glimpse of Him.

The God I hope you have seen is not a God of religion but a God of relationship.

The difference is as great as one being an ocean and the other being a prison cell.

One is for enjoyment, while the other is as awful as it sounds.

Make no mistake.

The Enemy has seduced us into lockdown by shutting down our faith.

This reminds me of the time I got to go into lockdown inside a prison in Oklahoma. It was the most unsettling, eerie feeling. The room was cold, tiny, and dark. The door had one little bitty window for the guards to peek in on the prisoners, for keeping watch.

The sight was bone-chilling—leaving me to shudder.

Why in the world would they want to misbehave only to be sent here?

Doesn't freedom feel better than this?

Then it hit me.

Better to be imprisoned in the safety of aloneness than in captivity's chaos.

Have you been seduced into captivity, friend?

If so, hear God speak these words over you today—

"Come to Me. Come out of the prison. It's time, child."

I sure love you.

Erin's words flooded my soul—as he hugged me tight in the middle of our foyer.

This wasn't the first time I heard those words coming from my handsome husband's lips. By now, we'd been married seven years. Adding the time of us dating, we'd been together for nine years. I'm unsure how many times he'd told me he loved me before. Only this time it drenched my hungering soul.

Perhaps you're wondering, *What in the world was the problem?*

That's a great question. I'd likely ask it too.

The problem was my faulty belief system. I projected onto Erin my own feelings. In many ways, deep down, I still had parts of me that felt unlovable. If I didn't really love me—how could he? Do you know this feeling? Can you possibly relate?

Interestingly, I did the same with God too.

Thinking I was trash—and He wants me? Really?

Can you hear Him calling to you?

More than reading words on a page, is your heart feeling stirred by His presence?

He's calling out to you, dear one.

Maybe a faint whisper? Maybe a prick at your heart? Maybe a desire to cry?

What you're encountering is the presence of God—He's near to you.

If not a whisper or a pricking of the heart, then maybe a pang of anxiety? I get it. Remember, God scared me too. You're not alone . . . *You're tendering to love.* You're tendering to the One who chose *emptiness* to fill you.

> He *emptied* Himself by assuming the form of a slave, taking on the likeness of men. And when He had come as a man in His external form, He humbled Himself by becoming obedient to the point of death—even to death on a cross. (Phil. 2:7–8, emphasis mine)

Indeed, the perfect, holy, compassionate God of all creation humbled Himself into a womb. A pure womb—but a womb nonetheless. The Seedling Savior, the Author of Life, He subjected Himself to the process of formation within a womb—a womb He first conceived in His hands.

Have you considered how the Maker of Life humbled Himself, taking on the raw nakedness and neediness of a seedling in a woman's womb—a womb He created? Or have you considered the sacredness of our Lord being pushed through the birth canal and into a world of hungry bellies, dirty diapers, breast milk, and needing to be burped?

God had to wait for a diaper change. 'Til the people He formed in their mothers' wombs got a clue from her son's cries and said, "Joseph, would you see if Jesus needs His diaper changed? Perhaps that's why He's so fussy?"

Oh friend, the Enemy has duped us for far too long.

Satan cannot handle us getting a glimpse of our amazing God.

Did you know he wanted to be God?

Did you know there was a mess in heaven *first*?

The mess didn't start with us—no, no.

It started with Satan who was called *Lucifer*, a beautiful angel.

If you think you're a mess, get this: *Satan has us both beat by a long shot.*

Satan is real. Satan is dangerous. And Satan is determined to destroy lives too.

That's not all.

Satan salivates at keeping you and me far away and distracted from God.

Before time began, when Earth was barren of humanity and heaven was full of activity a battle was waged between God Almighty and one of His angels, *Lucifer.*

He was a beautiful angel by all accounts but swelled to explosive narcissistic measures—he blew up on God in a fitful rage fueled by pride, arrogance, jealousy, and insecurity. He wanted to be "like the Most High God" by conquering his rival and rendering Him defeated.

The prophet Isaiah catches us up on what happened in his namesake book:

> Shining morning star, how you have fallen from the heavens! You destroyer of nations, you have been cut down to the ground. You said to yourself: "I will ascend to the heavens; I will set up my throne above the stars of God. I will sit on the mount of the gods' assembly, in the remotest parts of the North. I will ascend above the highest clouds; *I will make myself like the Most High*." But you will be brought down to Sheol into the deepest regions of the Pit. (Isa. 14:12–15, emphasis mine)

Even Jesus referred to Lucifer's fall:

"He said to them, 'I watched Satan fall from heaven like a lightning flash.'" (Luke 10:18)

Obviously, things didn't pan out so well for old Lucifer. He was thrown out of heaven and onto this earth—he and a third of heaven's angels who joined him in battle. Satan didn't know Who he was messing with, obviously. Through the death and resurrection of Christ, "He disarmed the rulers and authorities and put them to open shame, by triumphing over them in him" (Col. 2:15 ESV).

Signed, sealed, and delivered. Our God is a boss.

Satan is a powerful foe—yes. But make no mistake. He's no match for our God Almighty. Nor will he ever be. Moreover, Satan's power is highly limited when it comes to God's people. Don't believe me? Read the first chapter of the book of Job. Satan had to ask for God's permission to mess with His beloved one. What we learn in Job's story is a profound comforting truth in a set of devastating circumstances. If God agrees by giving Satan limited access—it's never to destroy us. It's to bring forth a radiant work of God in the midst of our allotted firestorm. We can rest our weary head on this foundational truth: Our God never ceases to reign in all power, all dominion, all authority—steeped in love.

However, we must know this—

As God's archenemy, the most proficient way Satan lashes back is by wreaking havoc on what God cares about most—His beloved children. The children He breathed life into and made for His pure enjoyment. Indeed, we are the ones He graced Earth to die for and now He joyfully lives in us. If you've received Jesus as your Lord, I hope you're feeling uniquely special. *Because you are.*

Not only that, *have you ever considered how special God must be too?*

Think about it.

God must *really* be something for Satan to covet Him like he did.

I mean, really.

Is not imitation the ultimate form of adoration and praise?

Does it not speak of a personal affinity?

Sans, Lucifer. A most privileged angel in his own right.

Beloved of God—His treasure.

What sickens me is to think the ugliness I see in myself is found in Satan too.

For example, if I'm feeling uncharacteristically insecure in who God has made me to be, Satan was too. That's how we landed in this whole ugly mess to begin with.

What is more, when I have, at times, freakishly wigged out by obsessively comparing myself to others, Satan did this too. That's why he raged jealously at God.

But that's not all.

When I nurse a compulsive need for praise and adoration in order to bring solace to my fleshly "all about me" side, Satan did so too.

How's that for wanting to throw up?

Satan's goal was to become the center of heaven's attention. You better believe he was hoping all of heaven's angels would soon bow at his feet and call him God.

But God wasn't playing that game.

Satan may have turned heaven and earth upside down for a limited slice of Earth's time, but God is still God. When we run to Him we are snatched from Satan's kingdom of darkness and Satan no longer has run-of-the-mill access to us. Neither are we bound to his kind of emotional activity. The Lord gives us a way out by His Spirit's work in us.

When we lean into the presence of God we find a release from the emotions originating in sin. That's why our Lord is happy to fill us with His peaceful security and stabilizing love. He hasn't a mind to withhold of Himself from those who look to Him. He's gracious, and loving, and kind in all of His ways.

Indeed, it is a lie of the Enemy for us to think of God as anything other than a rescuing, redeeming Father. If God's wrath is released against us, it's because we have chosen to take sides with Satan. And, honestly, how can we blame Him?

All I know is . . . I'm thinking God must be a boss. Are you?

I'm thinking God is all that and *more*—beyond anything we can imagine.

Here's what else I'm thinking: *Satan is highly fixated on us not seeing God.*

I honestly believe this is why scores of us struggle so hard in this journey of seeing and seeking our Savior. People often tell me stories about how they've tried to walk with God but when they do, everything in their life comes crashing down. As if walking with God makes everything in their life worse. I shake my head in frustration. I know exactly what they mean. I've been there myself. I know who's behind it.

But you and I don't have to put up with this.

Would you mind if I got fairly candid with you?

As much as I've begged God on your behalf to do a mighty work in you, I know it takes a willingness on your part. All of us must come to our wits' end, to a place of throwing ourselves at our Savior's feet and earnestly crying out for His help. *Giving Him our very life.*

Where we're so sick of this emotional prison and desperate for His immediate help . . . Where the world's delicacies, though once sweet, are becoming quite sickening now.

I cannot imagine a life of messiness is what you envisioned for yourself growing up.

No—this is not the life you envisioned for yourself. I don't believe it at all. What I believe is, this is the life the Evil One envisioned for you because he hates your life's purpose, to walk with God. God destined you for this life long ago, my friend. In whatever path you take, this is how God has wired you to glorify Him.

Do you not see it?

Has the darkness so shrouded your view?

If so, I beg of you to please allow me to speak life back into your precious ears.

Will you please allow me the place and space without throwing up walls?

I have no desire to preach at you or to you—no. I only desire to call you back to your heart's true home—to what you've known in the past and found to be assuredly true. I think you know you've lost your way in this battlefield of life. But that's okay. We all do from time to time. There's no stone to throw. When we've lost our way we need those who love us to remind us of what we cannot see, what is really true. Especially when the brokenness of our life is eating us alive.

Please hear me when I say this to you: You are fighting messiness, yes. But you are not just in this place because this is how life is. You are here because the things you have done with your life concerning your faith in Christ have ticked the Enemy off. He came after you, dangling just the right kind of bait before you, because this is what's true: From a seedling in your mother's womb, God set you apart for Himself. You also had a special gift on your life for accomplishing God's work in people's lives. You were called by birth to accomplish good works (see Eph. 2:10). And the Devil took note, I promise you. You threatened his work in destroying lives. If this were not so, why do you think you struggled so much to connect with God?

But he didn't stop there.

He also brought about an onslaught of continuous lies to slowly try to destroy you. And what's his greatest tool for destroying us? Is it not to convince us to wander off into acts of self-destruction by arousing in us strong desires for the forbidden which leads to hiding, secretiveness, and shame?

I believe so. And before we know it, we're struggling with severe bouts of insecurity, rejection, loneliness, fear, anger, bitterness, and resentment. At some point we began entertaining the lies: *Wow, you're a mess. See, no one loves you. See, no one cares for you. See, you don't matter. See, life isn't worth living. See, God doesn't really love you. See, you're nothing but a [you fill in the blank].*

If we come into agreement with these lies, we'll keep giving ourselves over to anything and everything self-destructive because we think, *Well, why not? I'm not worth much anyway? Besides, I'm just going to do it this one time. After that I'll stop.* But what's the end result? We feel even more out of control—more ashamed, more disgusted, more sick of ourselves.

Satan is a master at talking us into self-destructive situations. Then he turns on us by spewing loads of wicked condemnation onto us afterward to keep the torment fed . . . so the vicious cycle continues. Oh, friend. I have danced with the Devil too many times to not recognize how he moves. This vicious cycle has been my home at certain times in my life, and I know how awful it feels. The powerlessness, the ongoing defeat, the overwhelming hopelessness—it's smothering. We feel helpless, like we'll never overcome.

But these feelings are not the truth or end-all.

We may have found ourselves in the darkest pit of our lives, yes. We may have made a lot of mistakes we wish we hadn't, yes. We may be bound in serious addictions we wish we weren't, yes. But Jesus came to set us free from everything that holds us in captivity. With God's help, we can arise from the darkness. We can overcome. We really can rebuild the ruins and devastation. But we must lay down our lives before Him, surrendering our guts out to His lordship, and give Jesus something to work with—our real willingness to be helped. We must fall into His arms like little Baby C did into mine so the Miracle Maker can restore our smile, so He can heal us, and so He can help us to walk in true wholeness.

Can I tell you something? I long to see God do this in your life. Why not let Him right now? Why wait to surrender? Why wait to come back home? Why not let Jesus heal? Lift up your face to Him. Cry out for His help. He's waiting for you. He loves you so very much. He has a gorgeous plan for your life. He'll forgive, He'll cleanse, He'll restore every broken place and set you free. You've not gone too far. You've not out-sinned His merciful grace. Lay down your hurt, lay down your pain, lay down your anger, lay down your fear, lay down your disappointments. . . . Give it up to the One who can take it and do something with it. You will find nothing but love in your Savior's eyes. The kind of love you've longed for your whole life. The kind the Enemy has talked you out of. This you must know: you were born into this world so deeply loved, so deeply adored, and so deeply wanted. But did you also know as a tiny child the Enemy has sown seeds into your life so you would feel insecure, unloved, neglected, and like you didn't measure up?

The Lord has fought hard for you. But the older you got the harder it got. You didn't want to hear it. You began to pull away. And life got hard. But Jesus does indeed break our chains. He broke mine.

Why not let Him break yours too?

You've got so much life ahead of you to live. Good life!

Run to Jesus, friend.

One way we run to Jesus is by hollering out for Him with all of our might. A few winters ago our family took a ski trip to Utah. My firstborn had invited a college friend to join us for the week. Our lodging was quite far from the airport, and Peyton's friend's flight was several hours after ours, so I got the bright idea to schedule her a shuttle. What could go wrong? The signage claimed "easy, comfortable, and on time" service. So I phoned her and explained how it would work. She needn't worry!

When my phone rang at 11 o'clock that night I began to inwardly panic. The shuttle service had dropped her off at the wrong address. In freezing cold temperatures. With no idea where she was! So she commenced to knocking on doors. But everybody in the units were tourists—no one knew how to help. That's when I ran to the car in my flannel pajamas. Erin, Peyton, and I piled in. Peyton kept Shannon on her phone while I tried using Google Maps on mine. But we soon ran into another problem. Being in the mountains, the cell range was spotty. Just when we'd hear a possible address to come to, the call would drop, the phone would freeze or die entirely. When we couldn't call 911, I turned frantic. Every condominium looked the same at night. That's when we did what seemed best: We rolled down the windows of the minivan, honked the horn incessantly, and screamed out while racing down the streets, "Shannon, can you hear us?" Luckily, we found her an hour later.

Deep sigh.

I believe many of us could say our relationship with God has felt a little like this scene in the mountains. God is out there. We just can't find Him. And we're frantic. We pray but the connection seems spotty.

It's dark.

It's cold.

And we need help.

And Jesus says, "Give Me your life. Your *everything*. Bow down. Be still. Look up."

Another way we run to Jesus is by throwing ourselves into His Word afresh. By not allowing Satan to seduce us to an aimless faith by enticing us to be choosy saints.

Perhaps this story will help you to see what I mean.

My tenderhearted firstborn has a penchant for homeless people. When she abruptly announced to our table, "I'm taking my fries to that man!" I immediately thought to myself, *Yep, that's my girl.* Seeing Peyton's sudden feelings for the poor, and her obvious desire to do something about it, shocked our friends, I think.

Then, when the man devoured the fries, I had to resist the urge to gawk.

I was dumbfounded by how hungry he was.

I pulled my wallet out for Peyton to buy some more.

Peyton hightailed it to the counter and gladly ordered him a full meal deal. We were beyond happy as we anxiously awaited his order; even fearful that he'd wander off. Then, all the sudden, the homeless man did the inconceivable. He pulled out a full pack of cigarettes and fired one up.

You'd have thought someone slapped my girl right upside the head. Peyton has no patience for ill-gotten sympathy and she fumed that he was asking for handouts while smoking a cigarette.

All to say, he never did get his food.

Which left us in a quandary. What do we do with this food?

Suddenly Peyton remembered another homeless woman she had seen while walking from the parking lot to In-N-Out Burger.

Hurriedly, we headed her way and were delighted to discover she was *still* standing there. Yay! The food wasn't for naught after all!

Jesus' words—"For I was hungry and you gave me something to eat; I was thirsty and you gave me something to drink" (Matt. 25:35)—flashed through my mind. By then, Peyton had handed me the food and I simultaneously offered it to the lady while asking nicely, "Ma'am, are you hungry? Would you like some food?"

If I'm lying I'm dying . . . the lady replied, "I don't drink soft drinks," and enthusiastically took the food.

You'd have thought someone slapped *me* upside the head. Hold up.

Wait a minute.

What did you just say?

Her selectiveness sounds rather ridiculous but it did get me thinking: Isn't this how we, as Christians, are sometimes?

Taking the burger and fries of Christianity only to leave the drink? Jesus' blood on Calvary purchased our "Full Meal Deal" of redemption. Yet, our actions sometimes quip, "Thank You, Lord, but I don't drink obedience."

One reason our lives are messy and lack the New Testament power the disciples walked in is because we've gotten too choosy.

What if we started acting on God's Word?

What if we fully gave ourselves to becoming worshipping warriors?

That's what I see in the lives of the post-Pentecost apostles.

When the Lord they'd spent all that time with came to live *in* them . . .

That changed *everything*.

Come on—why not let it change everything in us too?

WHeRe We ARe
NOt ABLe-
God IS ABLe
WHeRe We CAN't-
OUR
god
>>> CAN <<<
#MORE

chapter eight

COME BACK

Two years ago I found myself standing on a beach and begging God to spare a stranger's life—for him to live and not die and declare the works of the Lord. The man was from Canada and, sadly, he had drowned. His wife and teenage sons were a stone's throw away from him in the sand as a group of men were feverishly trying to resuscitate him.

Horrifyingly shocked, they kept asking me, "Is he going to be okay? Please tell me he's going to be okay?"

I knew something they didn't—he had died already.

All I could do was clutch onto them and cry out to God.

Hundreds of people stood around gawking as if it was no big deal that people's lives were being ripped to shreds right there in front of us.

Gratefully, I was not alone in comforting the wife and children. Another woman had come as well—a Catholic sister. When I dropped to my knees to comfort the family, she grabbed onto me as if to say, "Yes! Thank you for coming! Please pray!"

And pray I did—from my guts I started crying out: "God, do a miracle! You have all power, authority, and ability! These oceans have boundaries because of You! These skies—You spoke them into being! You formed our bodies. You can resurrect them!"

As a group of men, total strangers, were thrown together in desperation to try to save this man's life, the Catholic sister and I were thrown together too, to minister in Jesus' name.

I was thoroughly unprepared for what God would lead me to do that day.

As I helped the family, I sensed God probing my heart.

Do I believe what I read in my Bible?

Of course I do, Lord!

Do I believe what I taught my class for two years from the Gospel of Luke? Do I believe God still desires to save, to deliver, to heal, and to bring the dead to life? Do I believe He wants His people to come back to the basics of their faith? Worshipping Him, walking with Him, hearing Him, and doing what He says?

Time stood still. I was undone. My head spun. It seemed as if God was calling my faith into utmost account. Line upon line and precept upon precept. I felt stripped naked.

I felt stripped naked as some very familiar words spoken by my dearest mentor reverberated throughout my mind:

Do I believe God is who He says He is?

Do I believe I am who God says I am?

Do I really believe the Scriptures I teach to others?

Will I walk forth in them in fullness of faith? Fullness of trust? Fullness of power and boldness? Unafraid of people and their reactions? Following wherever He leads?

Suddenly, God prompted again—

I felt Him urging me to pray for the man to come back to life.

Yeah, I know. It was nuts.

As hundreds stood about, I stretched out my hands over him and in a fairly loud voice began saying earnestly, "Come back in Jesus' Name. Come back in Jesus' Name. You shall live and not die—to declare the works of the Lord" (see Ps. 118:16–18).

Regrettably, the man did not rise from the dead. However, God used this tragic situation as a mile marker in my own life. Strangely, it proved to be a precursor to the bottom falling out in my life; to a time of God showing me how much I'd fallen captive to the deadness of dull, lethargic religion. Through this experience my own faith would receive some serious CPR. Interestingly, the verse I quoted over the man would be a word not only for me; I believe God means it for you too. "The power of the LORD has won the victory; with his power the LORD has done mighty things. I will not die, but live, and I will tell what the LORD has done. The LORD has taught me a hard lesson, but he did not let me die" (Ps. 118:16–18 NCV).

Obviously, I needed a holy shaking to wake back up to life in Christ. These are kind of hard lessons to come by, but they produce resurrection life afterward.

A life of living the words of the Bible, not just reading or quoting the words of the Bible. A life of not seeing people, as my friend Staci says, "as only landscape in my peripheral vision. But a life of coming back to the basics of my faith where I would take time to care, and share the love of Christ with people, anytime and anywhere, by sharing my own life—freely and fully.

When I first met Jesus, everywhere I went I told people about Him. I couldn't shut up over what He'd done for me. Oh, the satisfaction and peace! I was smitten by Him. His presence took my breath away. And I shamelessly told my testimony to anyone who was willing to listen. I couldn't believe God would love someone as wretched as me.

When the Lord said to love those who abused me, I did.

And forgave them too.

When the Lord said to share my testimony at my church, I did.

Over three hundred women came, God's presence was evident, and there wasn't a dry eye anywhere, and afterward the altar was full of women.

When the Lord said go up to random people at Walmart, Subway, Gold's Gym, or at the grocery store, I did.

There's no telling how many people came to Christ back then.

In fact, I had a neighbor who was just as much of an evangelist as me. She had the biggest passion for souls. She hardly ran a single errand without introducing people to Jesus. Patti *always* entered Jesus into the conversation. And, surprisingly, people opened up their lives to her instantly! If they had troubles, Patti listened to them. If they had questions as to the validity of God, Patti answered their questions the best she could from her heart. Come to think of it, I never remember seeing Patti read one commentary or doing any in-depth Bible studies. She wasn't really the intellectual scholarly type. But her love for Jesus was fierce and her acts of faith were profound. She was glued to her Bible every day. And talking to God in prayer for her was commonplace. She listened for God's voice, and obeyed when He spoke.

If God told Patti to do something, she did it.

If God told Patti to speak to someone, she spoke.

Patti exuded a winsome boldness, and people were attracted to it.

Mind you, the woman never minced words.

Who knows how many women Patti reached for Christ?

I remember people giving their lives to Christ in Walmart—weeping for the Lord.

Then, we'd bring them to my house so I could begin to disciple them in their newfound faith. Those were crazy times. Fun times. Jesus was showing Himself all around us.

But that's not all.

God was moving in lives all around.

Our lost friends were coming to Christ.

Our family members were coming to Christ.

We even walked the streets of downtown Houston ministering to people and loving on people. The homosexual community, the homeless community, and the street kids—you name it. We did it. And God worked wonders.

But somewhere along the way I got so busy inside the church walls that I stopped connecting with people outside the church walls. Not only that, somewhere along the way I began realizing in some parts of the religious world people with backgrounds like mine weren't so welcome to openly share where we'd come from in church settings.

Believe it or not, a dear friend of mine was asked by her women's director back then to speak at her church's women's retreat. But the director had one stipulation: I'd love for you to speak for us but can you please keep "certain things" private?

Imagine my shock when her "certain things" held no comparison to my junk.

Certain things like getting pregnant outside of marriage as a Christian.

My heart broke for her because, honestly, God used her junk to help encourage me in my newfound faith. This was definitely the beginning of my witness of Jesus slowly growing silent.

Satan knew exactly what he was doing. It's exactly what the apostle Paul warned the Corinthians of when he said, "But I am afraid that as the serpent deceived Eve by his cunning, your thoughts will be led astray from a sincere and pure devotion to Christ" (2 Cor. 11:3 ESV).

I was led astray alright.

Years later I would see how this silence brewed a slow burning fire of resentment in my bones that would come to burn me alive later on. First, I started resenting God for not giving me a prettier testimony. Then, I began resenting the church as a whole for silencing people's testimonies. Last, I began resenting myself for being a low-life, a willing contributor to my own sinful parts of my testimony.

What happened ever so slowly was this: My whole life was set aflame with a bitter root of resentment. I didn't even know it. All I knew was, I was slowly growing suspicious of people's motives, isolating myself, and suffering bouts of depression. I became extremely sensitive, often crying over anything and everything.

Not only this—

I began running from the call of God on my life.

Instead, I sought shelter, safety, and a life of simplicity and cushion—even despising, at times, the ministry God called me to. As if God was picking on me.

It all sounds so ridiculous, I know.

Then God allowed Satan to sift me like wheat similar to the apostle Peter:

> "Simon, Simon, look out! Satan has asked to sift you like wheat. But I have prayed for you that your faith may not fail. And you, when you have turned back, strengthen your brothers." "Lord," he told Him, "I'm ready to go with You both to prison and to death!" "I tell you, Peter," He said, "the rooster will not crow today until you deny three times that you know Me!" (Luke 22:31–34)

Talk about a season of tormenting doubt! I don't ever want a redo.

I thought I'd never recover from it or ever find my legs again. Shoot! Who am I fooling? I'm still in the process of recovering. But, you know what? All that junk needed sifting. It was killing my faith.

Not only my faith, it was killing *me*.

ℰ⁀

God is so good. Get this—

This past week at Hobby Lobby, I found myself acting like I did back in the early days of my faith, like Patti and I did with the cashier. Somehow I entered Jesus into the conversation, and learned the woman had recently fallen on hard times, just lost her home, is a single mom of a fifteen-year-old son, and absolutely loves her customers. By the end of our time together, I invited her to join me at church and gave her my number.

I haven't heard from her yet, but that's beside the point. More than anything, I'm just craving to be more like my old self again—the days of Patti and me.

I don't want to see people merely as landscape in my peripheral vision.

I want to burn with a love for Jesus and His people and souls.

So much so, I can't help but take the time to care, take the time to listen, take the time to speak up, and take the time to overtly share the wonder of the Good News.

I believe God is doing a new thing in the church today. This new thing is taking us back to the former things—akin to biblical days. Where the people of God love Jesus enough to share Him with a lost and dying world. Where we're so taken by Jesus, we cannot help but to speak of Him wherever we go. Where we are a little more transparent with our own stories and struggles because we understand *this* is what reaches people. Where we love people with all sincerity. Snatching people from pits of destruction because we burn with a passion for people's souls.

Where we hear God's voice and flat-out obey Him.

Where we're glued to the Scriptures *daily* and in constant prayer.

Where we say to friends after running some errands, *"You wouldn't believe who I met today and what God did!"*

Lately I've been thinking about how you and I don't need one more commentary, one more seminary degree, or one more Evangelism Explosion class to live the life God has called us to live by being a witness for Him. Just pull up your sleeves. Testify to God's goodness in your pain. Be loving, be merciful, be caring. Although all of these resources are wonderful, excellent, and worthy of value, they do not qualify any of us before God for kingdom works.

A seminary degree does not make the Devil run—a sold-out surrendered heart does. A polished and primped prayer does not make the Devil run—a believer understanding their authority in Christ and boldly declaring God's Word in prayer does. A life full of God's Word in our head does not make the Devil run—a believer who speaks it as truth does.

This reminds me of an experience I had in Africa a few years ago.

I was praying for a young girl—asking God to do a beautiful work in her life—when all of a sudden she began trembling violently. She was not in her right mind and was terrorized by what appeared to be an evil unseen presence.

At times she would fall into a deep sleep, almost dead like. Other times she would cry out. In the end, the Holy Spirit led me to pray for her and her entire family line, a prayer for their repentance and salvation. I did not understand it (I still don't), but I obeyed what I was sensing the Holy Spirit leading me to do. After doing so, praise God, she awoke, and she was gorgeously set free! Everyone in the room was slack-jawed and amazed by the Lord. With our own eyes we got to see the power of the Good News of the gospel breaking her wholly free.

Come to find out, her uncle was a witch doctor, and she was terribly afraid of him.

Knowing this, I immediately began teaching her about her God and how to do battle against the Devil. I told her she did not have to fear this uncle anymore. Christ lived inside of her now and He holds all power and authority over the Devil. All she had to do was to entrust her whole heart and life to God and God would protect her. In fact, I even told her, "If your uncle ever comes back around and tries to scare you or intimidate you, you look him straight in the eye with full courage in your God. Do not allow him to intimidate you. As you look at him, begin to pray to the Lord. Ask the Lord for His promise of protection over your life. Ask Him to protect you from the Evil One. And you keep praying until your uncle relents."

Would you believe the uncle came to her house that night?

He hadn't been around in ages either.

When he started staring at her in the scary way he had before, she stared right back as if to say to the evil presence in his life, "I am not afraid of you. God is with me and you cannot have me or harm me." She did not back down or quit praying until he looked away.

Do you know he looked to the ground and never looked her way again after that?

My friend, it worked!

When she came running to me the next day at camp, we rejoiced.

I was overcome by how sweet God was to teach her how to fight before I left.

Surely God did that while I was still there to build up her faith and to show her His power and authority as her heavenly Daddy—now living inside of her.

As God's beloved children, we can overcome forces of evil coming against us. Whether we are feeling like the little girl—all bound up—or simply feeling a deep resistance in our life toward God. We can experience a powerful release. The greatest weapons we fight with are wholehearted surrender to the Lord, prayer, and the Holy Scriptures.

Surrender brings us under the Father's authority and protection.

Prayer is our lifeline of communication with our Father.

The Holy Scriptures are God's promises to us and our way to know God's truth.

Listen, my friend:

Where we are not able—God is able. Where we can't— our God can.

He's our Helper, and Healer, and Comforter, and Counselor, and Holy Reminder.

He leads and instructs and teaches and trains.

We can trust Him to give us the answers.

We can trust Him to lead us and not leave us because He's moved in to stay forevermore.

Nothing can separate us—not even our own stupid, foolish, and sinful wrongdoings.

ℰ⌒

How about we take the land back that God has given us?

What is the land? Is it not the land of promise—the land of unbroken fellowship?

Walking miracles are those who are brave enough to take the Lord's hand to rise up from death to life. Into a life of living according to the leadership of our everyday Redeemer.

Would you like to know where our everyday Redeemer plans on taking us? Our everyday Redeemer plans on taking us to the land of promise: The land of everyday redemption.

Oh friend, do you see it?

Messes become miracles when God's people take His hand, rise up from sin's paralyzation, and walk in the fullness of the everyday Redeemer's abundant life. Instead of being the daughters of Eve and the sons of Adam who walked into deception, took the bait, and shared death with one another, we have the gorgeous gift of being the reborn daughters and sons of God. We are children who walk in the paths of God, protected from the deceiver in this broken garden of life.

Not only do we dine on the tree of life, we become oaks of righteousness that now live to share the life-giving food we have found in Christ with others. We share so they, too, can come back to life from spiritual death like we have, and it's Christ's love within us compelling us.

This reminds me of Mrs. Kitchen, the woman I spoke of in the first chapter.

When I was nine years old or so we moved to Texas, to the southeast side of Houston—a rougher area of town. Mrs. Kitchen was an elderly woman who, compelled by the love of God, befriended several of us children in the neighborhood, inviting and driving us to church. Never had I met someone like Mrs. Kitchen—so kind and nice. If perfect love can seep from pores, it seeped from hers.

Over the course of the next three years, I hopped into Mrs. Kitchen's car on Sunday mornings, Sunday nights, Wednesday evenings, and in the summers for Vacation Bible School at Meadowbrook Baptist Church. Nothing was as exciting as awaiting her arrival to pick me up. Her company to me was so safe, so comforting, and so lovely. I like to say, *She fed me Jesus.* Sadly, we moved away from her when I was twelve years old, but I always carried her memory close to my heart.

You might like to know that years later as a young wife and mom I contacted Meadowbrook Baptist to see if I could find her. She did not attend church there anymore but they were able to get her contact information for me. I was nearly shaking when I dialed her number. When she answered the phone with her beautiful Southern accent, I was instantly undone. I had to force these words out amidst a catharsis of tears:

> *Mrs. Kitchen, this is Tammie. The one you took to church all those years ago. I'm calling you to tell you thank you. Thank you for showing me Jesus. I love Him today. So does my husband. And I'm raising daughters to love Him too. Jesus has worked miracles upon miracles.*

After we gathered ourselves and quit crying, she joyfully told me stories about our times together I hadn't remembered. "Tammie, I'd come to get you and you'd be dressed and ready for church while everyone else in your house was still sleeping. Do you remember? I think God honored your heart to come to church—even when no one else joined you."

I marveled fresh over it—I'd not considered that before.

For years I thought it was her I was most attracted to. But looking back, it was her God.

Today I am endlessly grateful for her willingness to open up her life and busy schedule to me, a seemingly insignificant girl from a terribly broken home.

I feel the same way about Curtis and Julie. Each of these people lived a purposeful life, and were willing to open up their lives to a couple of young kids who had nothing to offer back.

But this is what the love of God does to people: It compels us to lovingly share our lives.

His life, really.

Remember when God asked why I was stealing His glory and then why I was not telling what He had really done for me? The devastation His words brought to my entire life were excruciating because, basically, God was calling me a thief. Not only a thief, but a thief who was blatantly squelching His redeeming light by hiding it, denying it, and silencing it from going forth by not bringing His life and hope to others.

Through this season with God I have learned a few critical things.

Our life is not our own to package how we want.

Our life is God's personal work of redemption and is not ours to stand in authority over.

In fact, our life is not ours at all. . . . Our life is His witness of His love, His redemption, and His life that He has entrusted to us to give away.

Did you know your life was meant to reveal the secrets of how God's kingdom works in the lives of broken, messy people? Have you ever thought of your life as something God entrusted to you as a way to give people a peek into the kingdom of God? Indeed, your life is God's way of disclosing

the secrets of the kingdom—the otherwise unknown ways of
how our Father has loved us, wooed us into His arms of love,
forgiven us, healed us, and set us free.

Years ago, I learned something I have never forgotten
from a speaker's conference.

My mother-in-law saw God's calling on my life to public
ministry and felt like I should attend a speaker's retreat to
help equip me. Honestly, I wasn't crazy about the idea. It
seemed awfully presumptuous of me to do so when only a
few invitations had come in for me to speak.

Besides, I had no ambition to be a speaker. But, in the
end, it seemed right to do after talking it over with a loved
one in ministry, as well as bringing it before the Lord in
prayer.

That weekend would prove to mark me in ways beyond
comprehension.

I learned as a speaker that vulnerability is vital for connecting with people's hearts. If we lack vulnerability as a
communicator we can easily set up an air of piety and people
feel talked down to. Not only was that a great lesson for
teaching, it was a great lesson for life.

The power of God is released through our lives when we
risk vulnerability by, as the beloved Henri Nouwen would
say, "pulling up our sleeves and showing our scars." Then
testifying of our Redeemer's love. The power of God is also
released when we stretch out our hand to touch the brokenness of others, like Peter, and to lift them to their feet.

The beauty of the gospel is this: A miraculous God
stretched out His hand of redemption to a world of broken
people paralyzed in sin—people born into a bloodline of
godless heritage—to lift us up to become walking miracles.

WE CAN
Sit & Soak
IN   THE
B·O·U·N·D·L·E·S·S
beauty
OF   A   GOD WHO HOLDS
THE
WORLD   IN HIS hands
EVEN OUR Messed-Up
lives. #MORE

chapter nine

ALIVE & ATTENTIVE

Remember the girl in the mirror feeling nasty to the core?

Well, her opinion of God was correct—*partly*. He was holy alright. But perfect people weren't His only forte. God welcomes the most bedraggled among us; embracing us as His beloved children the moment we readily bow.

These days the nearness of His loving, forgiving, and abiding presence fills my soul with great joy. Nothing this world offers comes close to knowing Jesus personally, having His Holy Spirit dwelling on your insides. I'm coming up on twenty years since I first came face-to-face with Jesus Christ, and His abiding presence of love is still stunning to me.

Thankfully, it seems with each passing day I'm a smidgen freer than I was before, since the gaps of intimacy versus isolation between God and me are closing ever tighter.

Truth is, any step toward trusting an unseen God for this heart is a wonder.

Pains and aches and bruises and beatings from people who should've been trustworthy through my formative years rendered me severely walled and fearful.

I know I am a handful to love but I certainly don't want to be. I think that's why I've come to love God so much because He's never wearied, throwing up His holy hands, sick of my ways. Oh, others have. But He hasn't. He faithfully pushes past my insecurities with such a furious tenacity—sometimes it so catches me off guard I cry.

Indeed, God's love is sweet. Why do I run away?

When I was younger, I was rebellious and liked being hard to handle, difficult to love. I made inner vows often: I'd never *need* anyone. That's what you do when people prove unfaithful. It's a protective mechanism for a wounded heart and it ushers in safety.

Well, a sense of it anyway.

Isolation carries its own evil haunting, it's own prison. The lie is at least it comes from my own hand and not someone else's. But, seriously, it's madness.

I will have you to know God did a profound work in me the day I rocked Baby C back and forth so tight you would've had to literally peel back my love. As the tears streamed down my cheeks, my Savior gushed words of love as loud as a waterfall, yet as intimate as a whisper over my own cracked and waterless soul.

He loved me like this. And all the past, all the pain, it *did* devastate. Just like this one, the robbery and thievery wrought my soul, it's true. I don't have to hurry on to wellness because being a victim is unacceptable in my culture. I don't have to hurry on to wellness so as to forget what is behind, leaning into what's ahead. I don't have to hurry at all. He'll hold me as long as I need. *This* is His joy.

It's taken years of search and discovery to find understanding as to why I am the way I am—then to live a lifestyle of dying so as to find Christ's resurrection life. Being a dog returning to its vomit has no appeal to this heart of mine, so I pine on. Somewhere or another you realize survivorship kills, especially great relationships. Healing is worth the uphill battle of journeying the road to Golgotha when an empty tomb *always* awaits.

When it comes down to it, I never felt loved growing up. Not a healthy protective kind of love anyway. I was also the daughter of a stepfather and his family who tried to make me their own but for whatever reason couldn't ever fully go there. It landed me in a place of being deathly afraid of fake love—the kind in stance, and reason, and show, because one *has to*.

The good news is, I'm finally beginning to trust people more than ever. I used to think I'd wake up one day to a wonderfully constructed performance of love by my friends and family, one others saw and admired and smiled at, but wasn't real. If I didn't forcefully stand against it, it consumed me—even in my dreams. Perhaps this is why I was all the time asking my husband if he *really* loves me or saying in silly tones, "Tell me you love me . . . " Large portions of my heart believed him and wanted to be sure but there were teeny tiny slivers needing to hear it *again,* just once more.

I did this with God too.

Of course, I wasn't *always* this way—just on the days I felt a tad bit messy.

❧

I often wondered as a new Christian if knowing Jesus would wear old like everything else. I can tell you what I told a new Christian recently, "All these years later, Jesus *still* satisfies."

When someone continues to love you through the ups and downs and twists and turns, it's pretty irresistible. Not only that, when someone stays faithful when you've proven less than faithful, less than trusting, quite guarded, full of wounds, and terribly cautious in relationship, it's gloriously too much. The love of God is everything we run from but so desperately need. Like peroxide on a wound or the setting of a broken bone, encountering God is a divine terror leading to glorious healing. Most of us run like the wind away from God because His holiness scares us. Deep down in the shadowy fragments of our hearts—the parts we don't want others to see—we know something is broken, bleeding, and hopelessly unfixable. An ethereal emptiness looms over us. A bankruptcy of soul security and satisfaction cries out in the watches of the night. We might be able to save face in front of others, but there is no denying it. We are hungry. Like restless wanderers in search of a forever home, is the bent of all humankind.

Truth is, we cannot pick ourselves up from this pit of destruction because we are not meant to. And many of us have bloodied hands from all the scratching, pulling, and frantic clawing of unsuccessful, yet feverish attempts of trying.

Some of us feel ramshackled of mind for all the knowledge but we still lack the know-how. Staring at the walls and calculating just one more way to get out of this hellhole of a soul without the help of God can drive a person crazy.

I know. Not from head knowledge but from experience.

I also know what I failed to see is this: My lack of ability to save myself was the very gift of God delivering me unto eternal life. I needed to look up and find Him.

If we'll accept the glorious gift of letting go of all vain attempts of survivorship apart from God, we shall find the missing ingredient leading to what the philosophers describe as arriving to the leisure of life. What we are looking for is a relationship encompassing the Father, the Son, and the Holy Spirit of God.

But here is the big, nasty, bitter, medicinal pill we must all swallow to come into Holy Communion of Love Divine: The pathway to Life is found in our death—death to any and all vestige of self—where we have sought salvation apart from fully and humbly surrendering to God Almighty. Where we open our hands and relinquish any and all rights. Where we ditch any and all forms of spirituality rooted in self-reliance or good will.

In our day, spirituality is on the rise. But if we do not see ourselves as needy beggars at the mercy of God we are in dangerous waters and drowning in deception. Then shall our souls feel awash in rivers of glorious love because we have experienced that profound forgiveness of a Creator who is majestically sweet and satisfying to every hungry growling we have ever had.

What we cannot see is our failure to save ourselves is actually a beautiful treasure. The very thing God desires is to lead us into the arms of a loving God who longs to come to our rescue if we'll cry "Uncle" and throw up our hands in surrender. It courses through our veins. So why seek a God who willingly reinforces such maddening insecurity?

So what do we do? We take to our own brand of safety.

For some, it's self-reliance.

For others, it's spiritualism lacking one critical element: Surrender.

To see the Sovereign unveiled before us is to experience a devastation so utterly vexing it sends us to our knees or faces in reverent fear before Him. Why fear? Because reverent fear is the beginning of wisdom (see Ps. 111:10). To fear God is to have a deep and reverential accountability to His will and ways.

When I first noticed God pursuing me, I ran away—scared. The God of my own mind was fickle, demanding, untrustworthy, and preferred perfect people—Sunday-best kind of people—of which, I was *not*. I was the kind who mothers warned their daughters against as friends. A surefire corruption to any good morals or carefully crafted shiny pink reputations.

Years later I'd discover the glorious news that when I was at my worst, Jesus Christ willingly died for me. He's done the same for you too. What's wild is He offered His bloody and beaten body as a sacrificial offering to lift up our faith-less and sin-stained bodies, clothing our messy and messed-up lives with His stunning, scandalous love.

It's nearly too much to stand when you've come to know Jesus firsthand. By His saving grace, sinners are welcomed into the arms of a fascinating and forgiving Savior. All these years later, sitting in His embrace, drinking in His love, receiving His forgiveness, being washed in His grace—these never go threadbare. I might run away with a tinge of temporary insanity for a few moments, but on my return I'm always set back aright—safe and sound, quieted and reassured.

Then I'm happy I returned home.

So much comes to steal our affections—even religious life.

Then, when gazing upon the landscape of American Christianity, one is left to wonder sometimes, "Do any *really* love God?" The deep need we have for approval, for power, for satisfaction is met within the Fount that never runs dry, which is Jesus Christ. We're all looking for refreshment more than we're letting on.

I believe we are much too near-sighted in our vision of the world and the role we play in it. Though our personal worlds and crisis and plans take our time and seize us with force, God is up to much greater realities than our perceptions can fathom.

If we could see from God's perspective, I'm likened to believe our problems would downsize while our purposes upsize—even in our difficult seasons and situations.

Isn't this what we're all desperate for anyway?

Wisdom? Perspective? Leadership? Answers?

What if our answer has been before us all along?

In the presence of God—the One we spend most of life ignoring?

Little do we know, we are not the main characters in this redemptive narrative of humanity settled into this season of time between eternity past and eternity future. Our lives are a spec of minuscule dust in the grand story of the Majestic One who is God Almighty. The One who came to rescue the messy ones known as His created. The problem is most of us run from this One our whole lives—even while we sit in pews, take the sacraments, study our Bibles, and serve people in His name.

What is this? What has happened?

I'd say we've bowed down to the same tree Adam and Eve bowed down to: the tree of the knowledge of good and evil. We know so much but powerlessly live so little. We guard ourselves against evil but are powerless to overcome our inner torments and obsessions. We are tangled up to good things but not God things. We are full of angst because we have been bowing to the lesser tree instead of the Tree of Life, which is Jesus Christ, who gives abundant life to all who reject the ways of the world to become single-minded, wholehearted worshippers.

Some of us have bowed down to the tree of the knowledge of good and evil while reading our Bibles. We have become full of biblical knowledge but our personal lives lack the New Testament power that's available to us because we've made an idol out of the words instead of encountering Jesus' promise of life within its pages. For to read the Scriptures is to dance a new dance in the Spirit. Where we are pulled up from the ditches of apathy, lethargy, deceptive thinking, and worldly wisdom to a feast with the Author of Life—a spiritual celebration.

Not that we are taken from painful circumstances or removed from sufferings. That's hogwash. And a great deception from ancient days up until now. None of us arrive to a place of spiritual utopia where we have the fearlessness of all of the saints combined. Believing God to the uttermost as if we can operate in the powers of angels. This is a great deception—where man's faith begins and ends upon himself. Where we pull up our collar, puff out our chest, click the back of our heels before others, and get the applause of man for being so super spiritual.

No, we are tools of worship within God's shed. And our greatest joy and satisfaction comes not from being worthy of use. It comes from the beautiful touch of divine connection to the One who picks us up, dares to use us for His glory, and serve another in His name in some lovely way.

⌒

This morning I dressed for work all happy and excited. Today was not an ordinary day. I was heading to a Christian bookstore in order to meet and greet customers and do a book signing.

So, I grabbed myself a coffee and headed there.

Once the event came to a close, a woman looking around for a book caught my eye. I'm about as nosey as they come, and I sure was wondering what this twenty-something woman was looking for. I watched her pick up several books, read the back cover, then return them to the shelf. As I made my way over, we started talking. In the end, she was looking for something to connect her more fully to God and to find a sense of passion and purpose in her life.

Call me crazy, but I highly encouraged her to get a cheap paperback New Living Translation Bible, take it home, sit down, be still, and just read it to read it. Starting in the New Testament, while asking God to speak to her through His Word. I also told her a few more things.

- Your purpose in Christ is caught not taught—the Holy Spirit will lead you.
- Your passion for Christ is caught not taught—sit with Him, talk to Him, read His Word.
- The life you are longing for is found in the basics of a relationship with God: prayer, reading your Bible, surrounding yourself in a Christ-filled community, serving broken people, and worshipping Jesus from an obedient heart.

⌒

Truth is, moderation and balance are essentials in life. However, in respect to an active intimate relationship with God, our inner worship of Him should know no boundaries.

We are invited to throw our very lives lavishly at His feet—basking in the beauty of His holy, wonderful, and deeply satisfying presence. In His presence, every wrong and misguided motivation is met with clarity, guidance, fulfillment, and the tender counsel of a God who knows all things but never treats us as a know-it-all as if we're stupid. We are safe in His presence to ask dangerous and typically awkward questions because the One we ask deciphers our fears, frustrations, and reasons for asking before one word escapes from our lips.

When we come without caution, letting down our performance-based walls—we find a God who is ecstatic with joy. Finally! *My child is acting like My child—safe in his or her Father's presence.*

For in His presence, paupers find freedom to express themselves as victims without even so much as a flinch from their heavenly Daddy's face—He who knows all things doesn't question our words or motives. Instead, God comforts the wounded heart. Then, when He sees fit, He ushers in the tasty treats of truth. But never before its time. In God's infinite wisdom, He alone grasps the reality that we need comfort before we need truth. For whatever reason we're hurt, wounded, scorned, confused, misguided, full of messiness, hard for others to handle—God deciphers through the muck and mire to a heart that is crying to feel understood and accepted and loved, just as we are.

What we find in our Father's presence is:
God cares when others don't.
God cares when others won't.
God understands when others don't.
God understands when others won't.
God listens when others don't.
God listens when others won't.

❧

I have discovered much of our frustrations find rest if we'll take them to God before we take them to others. People cannot handle our brokenness and conflicted emotions most of the time. And we feel angst because of it. What words full of waste we spew on those who, on many days, are as equally conflicted as us—whether we can see it or not.

Jesus says, "Come to Me, all of you who are weary and burdened, and I will give you rest. All of you, take up My yoke and learn from Me, because I am gentle and humble in heart, and you will find rest for yourselves. For My yoke is easy and My burden is light" (Matt. 11:28–30).

Could His yoke be beautiful counsel?

Could His yoke be flagrant understanding?

Could His yoke be tender mercy or a compassionate ear?

Could His yoke be wise and intelligent direction?

Oh what fuss and fret and frustration we'd save ourselves if only we took all things to God in prayer. Oh what fuss and fret and frustration we'd save ourselves if we let down our walls and communed with God from a raw and real place and space. God is not looking for polished and primped prayers from our lips. With God we can forsake suits and heels for flip-flops and workout pants. God is holy but He is not stuffy. We are welcomed to dine with the King of kings as chosen children, not highly decorated, manners driven, buttoned up and beautifully dressed guests. Many of us are still messy because we haven't learned we can let down with God. We like others to think we are good people—maybe even activists in our communities and world—but we hardly know how to keep company with God. We've hardly moved from the socially awkward space of meeting and greeting and enjoying tea. God would love to welcome us for a weekend getaway where we sit and soak in each other's presence, talking and sharing stories for hours on end . . . But we keep making excuses because we're not so sure we'll enjoy ourselves.

To be honest, we've been uncomfortable entrusting ourselves in His company for *that* long. Surely you've gone somewhere only to find yourself wanting to leave but can't?

How about this one . . .

Have you invited guests over for a few hours only to inwardly wish they'd hurry up and leave?

I mean, better to not enter in than to find ourselves in a position of vulnerability, stuck somewhere because we're too afraid to tell our host we're ready to leave, right? We are vastly complicated creatures, aren't we? Way down in the raw places where our emotions are complex, we are a people deeply scared of entrusting ourselves to anything.

Unless we really are dog-tired or something, our restlessness stems from a disconnect in intimacy.

We, for whatever reason, cannot emotionally let down so as to feel at home.

Jesus is not this way.

The disciples were—they'd want to send the people away. But Jesus always felt compassion and cared for their needs. Even the little kids loved being with Jesus, and He welcomed them with tenderness and joy. But the disciples had to be told—don't shoo them away! Or how about the woman who was too much for society with her socially awkward ailments—she found validation and healing in Jesus' love, power, and personal touch. Even the hem of His garment was saturated in redemptive power.

Those in Scripture who were brave enough to seek, to throw themselves at Jesus' feet, to ditch religious and social norms, and to be near Jesus and touched by Jesus—these were the ones who experienced the profound blessing of the miraculous life. While some stood around sneering with judgment, others forsook such self-centeredness to dance, to leap, and to celebrate the glorious love of God wrapped in human flesh. That's what the desperate do when they finally find what they've been looking for their entire lives. What foolishness to call them weaklings in need of a crutch. Strength in God's eyes is not humanity being determined. Strength to God is finding Him lovely enough to fling wide our hearts while crying, "Here. Have Your way!"

We've been taught to believe we can do anything we want if we try hard enough. This is worldly wisdom that falls flat in the face of God. An audacious slap to God's holy face. Because, truth is, we are not in control—He is.

Now *faith* says, "I can do all things through him who strengthens me" (Phil. 4:13 ESV).

God Almighty is the beginning and end, the Alpha and Omega.

And when we entrust ourselves to an all-powerful God we are let off the hook of maintaining our muscles, keeping up such a valiant display of determination. There is no need to validate our existence or keep others impressed with our winsome personality. Instead, we can wake up to a new day of purpose and endless possibilities because God is our power supply and help, and His mind and power knows no end.

Do you see how different the approaches to life are?

One has self as the center of the universe.

The other has God upon the throne.

Seeing God as high and exalted is soothing for the soul who has entrusted itself to His loving, authoritative care. When we do, we have no worry of judgment. We can welcome His rule and reign in our life, knowing His miraculous power is available for our every mess—past, present, and future. We feel no need to clean ourselves up anymore. For we are freely drinking from the rich and satisfying river of grace where all are welcome. This is a beautiful place where all our thoughts are learning to begin and end on God.

What God thinks.

What God says.

What God knows.

What God feels.

When we don't know someone intimately we cannot go much deeper than small talk.

Who tells strangers their secrets?

Who tells strangers their fears?

Who tells strangers much of anything other than the time, a direction, or a negative vent?

But in the presence of God and His Word we know His thoughts. We know His ways of how He sees life and our place in it. We hear His heart, and how He feels about every-thing—*even us.*

Want to hear something wild?

Would you believe I was standing in front of my mirror getting ready when God led me to write this message? *I sure was.* For a long time I did not make the correlation. Then, I did.

Seeing ourselves the way Christ sees us is nothing short of miraculous.

I have a question for you.

What if you read the Bible not as a list of rules or regula-tions but as the wonderful, complex, transcendent happenings of God in ordinary messed-up lives? What if you read every demand for obedience not so much as a God who likes boss-ing you around but as a loving Father whose greatest desire is for you to become the beautiful soul He has made you to be? What if obedience was God calling you to rise up into the worthy vessel of value that God sees when He looks at you?

This begins and ends daily at the feet of Jesus.

In His presence we need not defend ourselves or pretend to know what we don't. We can sit and soak in the boundless beauty of a God who holds the world in His hands—even our messed up lives.

❧

This reminds me of a young woman I know who lives on the other side of the world.

Have you ever encountered someone so fascinating you could hardly describe in intelligible words what their presence evoked in your heart? Where the sheer beauty of their countenance sent your mind exploding with a volcano of thoughts, insecurities, and a heavy dose of fresh perspective in life?

That's what happened the day Beauty took to the platform in Lusaka, Zambia, and led several hundred of us in attendance in worship to God. As she held the microphone and joyfully thanked God for His love, His grace, and His mercy in our lives—she did so with fiercest passion as one who has experienced it firsthand. The girl's face was so bright it was as if a light was turned on inside of her. And her smile, oh, it assaulted my emotions. Because this is what I know about Beauty: she comes from an exceptionally broken life with more troublesome baggage than most will even know in their lifetime.

But her broken past has no hold on her present state in life or her future destiny. She is a miracle in the making because she has come face-to-face with a miraculous God who has wholly redeemed her life from an utterly ravenous pit.

Not only that.

Her sheer fascination with her God ignites a fresh fire in you to want more of Him too. Even if you already know Him—you want more.

Beauty undid me that day.

This was the same trip where I held Baby C in my arms.

Far too many circumstantial storms had taken a toll on my heart.

The cracks and booms of lightning and thunder and a torrential downpour of painfully pelting rain finally sent me to drowning in doubt—filled with despair. How could God allow such heartache to happen to us? Does He care?

God used Beauty to remind me of the beauty of His presence.

I have asked one thing from the LORD; it is what I desire: to dwell in the house of the LORD all the days of my life, gazing on the beauty of the LORD and seeking Him in His temple. (Ps. 27:4)

When had I forgotten life is hard but God is good?
What talked me out of remembering—
To give God my life is to enjoy the more I was made for.
Him.

❧

Oh friend, walking with God is so much more than boring obedience.

It's actually awakening to the One who holds the universe in one hand while extending the other to us—His beautiful creation—in wondrous grace and says to us, "Can I have this dance?"

Being the perfect Gentleman, He doesn't press us past the point of awkwardness. Whether we decline or receive His gracious offer, we have a sense of freedom to choose. Yet, many of us feel caught in a tailspin of conflict between taking His hand or not. If we're honest, some of us are mad for being put in this situation in the first place. Others of us have lived around this dance so long we're unmoved by it. Still others of us were raised to live so far above personal vulnerability.

Many of us think to ourselves, *Why on earth would I lower myself to such demonstrations of foolishness as dancing? People can do whatever they want but the only reason I even came to this dance was to appease the one who brought me here in the first place. Besides, isn't the people-watching great? Have you seen how some of these folks dance? To tell you the truth, I've worn embarrassment for them a time or two.* Then again, after going home, we must admit there's a

sliver of us who hates admitting we're a little jealous of those
who have such a carefreeness of heart out there dancing.

Hmmm. Do you ever wonder what life would be like
if we ditched our performance-driven living and ravenous
insecurities by throwing caution to the wind and downright danced? Danced until all performance-driven living
was shaken from its tight grip on our soul. Danced until we
quit caring so much about what other people think. Truth
is, maybe we should quit sitting around having theological
debates about such things as dancing. While the One who
extends His hand to us for a glorious dance is gracious but
we keep failing to take His hand.

Why is this so?

Why do we decline or even shift our eyes from His gaze
and shamefully say, "No. That's okay. I'm good, actually."
All the while we're secretly wishing we weren't so insecure to
look like a fool for some lighthearted moments of fun.

He's such a good dancer, we think to ourselves, *surely He
doesn't want to dance with me.*

The Queen of Misfits among such throngs of worthy
women?

This is when a sense of doom, gloom, and a critical spirit
arrests our thoughts.

We're trying to pretend we're good but our face is telling
on us. It always does.

Why can't we be perfect like the ones we've seen dance
with Him before?

Even more perplexing—why does He continue to dance
with those so seemingly self-righteous, judgmental, and
downright mean? Doesn't He discern such ugliness behind
each one's eyes? When He really looks at them?

Bewildered by it, I have had to fight off entertaining the
thought of walking away.

But suddenly and surprisingly a surge of something
lovely has hit me these days.

Perhaps it's time I quit refusing myself of what might do this soul some good?

Maybe this is the more I've been longing for?

Perhaps I'll find my legs?

I can see His hand.

It's outstretched my way.

Oh Lord, here we go—I'm going for it . . .

Wait, He wants you to come too!

Hurry now! What are you waiting for?

acknowledgments

Few will ever know the toll this writing took on a whole passel of my loved ones, faithful friends, gracious ministry partners, or me while God did His thing—*thank God!* To these beloveds I must publicly esteem for their private acts of spurring me on, praying me forward, and blowing wind into my sails when I wanted to quit. Each of you knows this message was brought forth in one of the worst seasons. How can I thank you enough for your love, prayers, and presence in our lives?

You are gifts of God's grace to me.

To Jennifer Lyell—Surely you know you hold a miracle in your hands? From start to finish, God used you to bring *More* forth. Not only do I admire, honor, and respect you deeply, I could burst for the gratefulness I feel for how you've believed in me. You have become more to me than my acquisitions editor—you're my friend.

To Jenni Burke—Can you believe this finally came to be? You deserve a weekend at the spa, my agent and friend. Thank you for holding my hand all along this rocky path, and for continually believing in me. Your love for Jesus is beautiful. Not only do I sing your praises, I love you.

To my B&H team—Because of you, this message is going forth. Jana, you are a rock star editor. Laurel, your design work is stunning and I know you will nail the marketing campaign. Diana, Jeff, Kim, and a whole host of others, you are a rock star production team. From designers, to copyeditors, to marketers, to sales and distribution, to whatever other hats you ended up wearing . . . because of all of you, this message is ready to go forth to those who are truly hungry for more. I esteem each of you so much.

To my dearest friends and ministry partners—What kind, patient, and crazy gracious treasures you are! Other than Erin and the girls, I'm certain none are more thankful this project was seen to the finish line than you. Forgive me for wearing you out over "the book." Others would steal you from me if they knew the treasure I have in you. *I adore you.*

To my beloved spiritual mothers and mentors—Beth Moore and Pat Hightower. Never in my wildest dreams did I fathom in my early twenties what you'd come to mean to me all of these years later. This life and ministry is an outpouring of your inpouring. Thank you for teaching me by example what a godly woman looks like wrapped in skin. Not only have you lovingly cleaned up my knees when I've fallen, you've spurred me on to keep going after the More I was made for. *I honor you so!*

To my faithful shepherds—Curtis and Amanda. Because of your bravery to follow hard after God in our day, I am following suit. You are worshipping warriors, and I'm grateful to call you my pastors. Your prayers have carried me this past year. Not only do I appreciate you, I love you both. *How's this for my own lane and a big cup?*

To my lovely daughters—Peyton and Savannah. Without your courage to approve of your momma telling her story, this message would not exist in writing. Savannah, I'll treasure forever the night you said to me, "Mom, people don't really believe people can *really* change. . . . You need to tell your story." Little did you know God would use those words to make me stand taller in trust. Same thing goes for you, Peyton. The night I stepped down from the platform at the BCR Women's Retreat and you said, "I'm so proud of you for finally telling it, Momma. It was really good! And I'm not just saying it because you're my mom," you breathed iron into my soul. I have no greater honor than being your mom. *No two girls are more loved by their momma than you.*

To my handsomest husband—the one and only love of my life. Where do I even begin, honey? All I can say is, I still feel like the luckiest girl in the world to be yours. You had me at the first wink . . . Has God not been so good to us? I'm not the only walking miracle here, you're one too. *This work is as much yours as it is mine.*

To my beloved Lord—Whom I love more than life itself. How have I been so blessed by Your continual pursuit of me, love for me, and patience with me? If any one soul could possibly wear You out, surely I have. But You've continued still. You are better than my human words can express. I sure hope the completion of seeing this thing through has brought joy to Your heart. It's all about You, Lord—what You can do in any life. Use it as You wish. I'm deeply honored to offer it up to You as my best offering in this season. *I love You.*

notes

1. See http://www.oxforddictionaries.com/definition/english/mess, "mess," accessed Sept. 22, 2014.

2. See http://www.oxforddictionaries.com/definition/english/miracle, "miracle," accessed Sept. 22, 2014.

3. A. W. Tozer, *The Pursuit of God* (Camp Hill, PA: Wing Spread Publishers, 1993), 36.

4. A. W. Tozer, *The Pursuit of God with Study Guide* (Camp Hill, PA: Zur Ltd. 1982, 1993), 95.

5. John Piper, *Desiring God, Revised Edition* (Colorado Springs: Multnomah, 2011), 10.